George Thacher Balch, Wallace Foster

A Patriotic Primer for the Little Citizen

An Auxiliary in Teaching the Youth of our Country the True Principles of American Citizenship

George Thacher Balch, Wallace Foster

A Patriotic Primer for the Little Citizen
An Auxiliary in Teaching the Youth of our Country the True Principles of American Citizenship

ISBN/EAN: 9783337306489

Printed in Europe, USA, Canada, Australia, Japan

Cover: Foto ©Paul-Georg Meister /pixelio.de

More available books at **www.hansebooks.com**

PRIMER

...TIZEN.

...Youth of Our Country
...of American
...

...er goes by, and reverentially bow or
...opportunity, for true
...an angels
—W. F.

INDIANAPOLIS:
LEVEY BROS. & CO., PRINTERS AND BINDERS.
1898.

INTRODUCTION.

OUR National Flag having been adopted as an auxiliary in instructing our youth in patriotism, and as a perpetual object lesson, it is necessary to introduce American citizenship, patriotic history, inspiring literature and music in the public schools if we desire to make our boys and girls good citizens and teach them loyalty and respect to authority and obedience to law.

We rejoice in the widespread interest our American educators and NOBLE, PATRIOTIC WOMEN are taking in the cause of intelligent citizenship by instructing our youth in American patriotic history. We believe from present indications the time is not far distant when every child in our land will receive its due share of patriotic instruction.

It needs no argument to prove that the perpetuation of our National life and institutions can be maintained only by inculcating in the minds and hearts of the rising generation the true principles enunciated in the Constitution and the Declaration of Independence.

Therefore, whatever we wish to see introduced into the life of a nation must first be introduced into the life of its schools. In view of this educational axiom, and with the hope of awakening a wider and more intelligent interest in the history of our Republic, we must increase our interest for a grateful, reverent admiration for God, our Country, our Language, and our Flag.

In consideration and in memory of the late Col. George T. Balch, the author dedicates the "American Patriotic Primer for the Little Citizen" to our BOYS AND GIRLS attending the public schools, with a fervent wish that their love for their country and flag may increase day by day and graduate them noble, generous, law-abiding, loyal American citizens.

W. F.

GOD WANTS THE BOYS AND GIRLS.

God wants the boys, the merry, merry boys,
The noisy boys, the funny boys,
    The thoughtless boys;
God wants the boys with all their joys,
That He as gold may make them pure,
And teach them trials to endure;
His heroes brave He'll have them be,
Fighting for truth and purity.
    God wants the boys.

God wants the happy-hearted girls,
The loving girls, the best of girls,
    The worst of girls;
God wants to make the girls His pearls,
And so reflect His Holy face,
And bring to mind His wondrous grace,
That beautiful the world may be,
And filled with love and purity.
    God wants the girls.

—[Anon

A PATRIOTIC PRIMER FOR THE LITTLE CITIZEN.

OUR COUNTRY.

1. What is the name of our country?
The United States of America.
2. Who govern in the United States of America?
In the United States of America in which we live and which is *our country*, we, The People, govern ourselves.
3. What are the principles on which government by the people is based?
The system of government by the people rests upon two great political principles, embodied in the DECLARATION OF INDEPENDENCE, at Philadelphia, July 4, 1776.
4. What great principles did the Declaration of Independence proclaim?
1. The right of the whole body of the people to govern themselves, to make their own government. 2. The equality of all men before the law.
The reason the people in these United States have for more than one hundred years successfully governed themselves is, that a firm belief in the justice of these principles has taught them to trust one another, has trained them to believe in one another, has educated them to respect the rights and the opinions of one another.
5. How does our Government differ from a Monarchy?
In the United States we have neither Emperor nor King, Queen nor Nobles. The people choose their own officers.
6. What is a Democracy?
A government of the people, by the people, for the people is called a Democracy. It is a government of the whole people by each one of the people deciding for himself what he will do or what he will not do.
7. What is a Republic?
When the people choose some person to stand for them, to do what they wish him to do, or to say what they wish him to

say, such a person is called their REPRESENTATIVE. All the representatives chosen by the people, taken together, make what we call the GOVERNMENT. Such a government is called a REPRESENTATIVE GOVERNMENT or a REPUBLIC.

8. What do we understand by States?

Large countries are usually divided for convenience of local government into several parts. In our own country these subdivisions are now forty-five in number, and are called States. Each State is a REPUBLIC having its own REPRESENTATIVE GOVERNMENT.

9. When was our Republic formed?

More than a hundred years ago, after the War of the Revolution.

10. What is the Union?

The uniting of several States into one country is called a Union. These forty-five American States have chosen to unite themselves in this manner. This union is called THE UNITED STATES OF AMERICA. Another name for it is the GREAT REPUBLIC.

11. When was the Union formed?

At the close of the Revolutionary War.

12. How many States formed the original Union?

Thirteen.

13. What were they?

New Hampshire, Massachusetts, Rhode Island, Connecticut, New York, New Jersey, Pennsylvania, Delaware, Maryland, Virginia, North Carolina, South Carolina and Georgia.

14. How were the other thirty-two States formed?

At the time of the formation of the Union several of the States owned large tracts of land that were but thinly settled, and other large tracts have since been acquired by the United States. As fast as portions of this country large enough for a State became thickly enough settled, a State government was formed and the new State admitted into the Union.

15. What is the Constitution of the United States?

The people of these forty-five States have entered into a solemn agreement, to establish a government which all will support, obey and defend; to do their business with one another and to regulate their conduct toward one another, and their conduct toward all other peoples in the world, according to the requirements of a document called THE CONSTITUTION OF THE UNITED STATES.

16. What is the Nation?

All the people living in these forty-five States, that is the sixty-seven millions of inhabitants in this country of ours, taken together, form what is known as THE NATION. In other countries the Emperor, the King or the Queen is known to the people as the SOVEREIGN, and in those countries the Sovereign represents the Nation. In the United States THE NATION IS THE SOVEREIGN, and this is why we often speak of the Sovereign People. In this country, therefore, the government is but the machinery through which, or by which, THE NATION rules.

17. What six objects are expressed in the Constitution of the United States?

THE AMERICAN NATION, speaking in all its majesty and power in this Constitution, says: "We, the people of the United States, in order to form a more perfect Union, establish justice, insure domestic tranquillity, provide for the common defense, promote the general welfare, and secure the blessings of liberty to ourselves and our posterity, do ordain and establish this Constitution for the United States of America."

18. When and where did the Constitutional Convention meet?

The Constitutional Convention met from May to the middle of September, 1787. The place of meeting was at Independence Hall, Philadelphia.

19. Why was it necessary to make a new Constitution?

Because the Articles of Confederation did not give enough power to the central government.

20. What leading men were most instrumental in bringing the Convention together?

Washington, Hamilton and Madison.

21. What was the character of the men composing the Convention?

The greater part of them were of Puritan ancestry; more than half of them had received a college education; all but twelve of them had at some time been members of the Continental Congress; eight had signed the Declaration of Independence; three had been members of the Stamp Act Congress;

Franklin, the oldest member, had been the leading spirit in the Albany Convention of 1754.

22. Where did they get the experience and wisdom that enabled them to make a Constitution so perfect?

From the time that the Puritans formed and signed the May Flower compact to the time when the Colonies became States, the people had discussed different plans of union. When the Colonies became States, the States formed constitutions for themselves. In making and working their State Constitutions the people learned what was needed for the Constitution of the United States.

23. Into how many and what departments is our government divided?

Our government is divided into three departments: Legislative, executive and judicial.

24. Of what does the legislative department consist?

The legislative department consists of a Senate and a House of Representatives and the two together are called the Congress. It is the duty of this department to make the laws for the United States.

25. Of what does the executive department consist?

The executive department consists of a President and Vice-President. It is the duty of this department to see that the laws of the United States are enforced.

26. Of what does the judicial department consist?

The judicial department consists of the United States Courts. It is the duty of this department to try persons accused of disobeying the laws of the United States, and to determine whether the laws passed by Congress are based on the Constitution or not.

27. What is the Supreme Law of the land?

The Constitution says: "This Constitution, and the laws of the United States which shall be made in pursuance thereof, and all treaties made, or which shall be made, under the authority of the United States, shall be the supreme law of the land; and the judges in every State shall be bound thereby, anything in the constitution or laws of any State to the contrary notwithstanding."

28. What was the War of the Revolution?

The American Colonies, thirteen in number, rebelled against Great Britain, in 1776, and proclaimed the Declaration of Independence and the right to govern themselves.

29. What were the chief causes of the Revolutionary War?

First—The right of arbitrary government claimed by Great Britain and denied by the Colonies.

Second—The influence of France, exerted constantly so as to incite a spirit of resistance.

Third—The natural disposition and inherited character of the Colonists, republican in politics and dissenters in religion.

Fourth—The growth of public opinion in the Colonies tending toward independence.

Fifth—The personal character of George III, altogether too despotic.

Sixth—The passage by Parliament of a number of acts destructive of Colonial liberty, resisted by he Colonies, and the attempted enforcement of these acts with the bayonet by Great Britain.

Seventh—The declaration by the Colonists of their complete independence from British rule.

30. What were the chief results of the war?

Independence of the Colonies and the formation of a new Nation.

31. What were the causes of the War of 1812?

First—The closing of the ports of Europe by England against American commerce.

Second—Impressment of American sailors of English birth, based upon the doctrine that a person born on English soil is an English subject. The United States claimed that men may give up their inherited citizenship and transfer their allegiance to other countries.

32. How was war declared?

By proclamation June 19, 1812.

33. When was the treaty agreed to?

December 24, 1814.

34. What caused the Mexican War?

FIRST—Mexico claimed Texas as part of her territory, notwithstanding its independence was acknowledged by the United States, England, France and other governments. The United States, by annexation, claimed the Rio Grande as the Texan boundary, while Mexico alleged the western limit of the province never extended west of the Nueces River. The crossing by General Taylor was considered the commencement of war, and Mexico made the attack.

SECOND—Impoverished by civil war, Mexico did not hesitate to replenish her treasury by plundering American vessels in the Gulf of Mexico, and also confiscated property of American merchants within her borders, covered by the treaty of 1831, but not lived up to.

THIRD—INTERNAL POLITICS, on both sides.

35. When was War Declared?

May 13, 1846.

36. When was the treaty agreed to?

February 2, 1848.

37. What caused the War of the Rebellion?

Conflict between the Free States and the Slave States, on the subject of States rights. This conflict culminated in the ELECTION OF ABRAHAM LINCOLN.

38. What were the costs of the Great War?

To maintain the Constitution in its integrity and to preserve the UNITY OF THE NATION thirty years ago, nearly five years of terrible war was fought, in which seven hundred thousand men laid down their lives that this Nation might live. So we see that this Constitution of the Nation is a very precious instrument to all Americans, a monument of human wisdom which this great Nation stands ready to-day, and will ever stand ready, to defend against the assaults of any power that dares meddle with or to oppose it.

39. What is a citizen of the United States?

This Constitution says that "all persons born or naturalized in the United States and subject to the jurisdiction thereof, are citizens of the United States and of the State wherein they reside."

40. How is a foreigner naturalized?

When a citizen of another country desires to become an American citizen and enjoy all the rights and privileges of such citizenship, he must declare on his oath " that he will support the Constitution of the United States, and that he absolutely and entirely renounces and abjures all allegiance to his former government and particularly to the prince or potentate whose subject he was.' He must further prove that he has lived within the United States for five years, at least one year in the State, and that he has borne a good moral character.

41. Can a citizen be of any color, race or religion?

A citizen may be of any color, may be born in any other country, or may be a Christian, a Hebrew, a Mohammedan, a Confucian or a follower of any other religion, or of no religion; so long as he obeys the laws, no matter what his color, his nationality or his religion, he is entitled to all the rights which citizenship confers (except the Chinese, who are excluded by act of Congress of 1882).

42. What is a little citizen?

Every little boy or girl born in this country, or if born in any other country, whose parents have been naturalized, is a LITTLE AMERICAN CITIZEN, who is learning every day how to be a big citizen. There are more than SEVENTEEN MILLIONS of SUCH LITTLE CITIZENS between the ages of three and fifteen years in the United States to-day.

43. How do the citizens govern?

The citizens govern either by voting for the person whom they wish to represent them, or who will say what the people wish him to say, or by voting for that thing which they would like to do or to have done, or against that thing which they do not wish to do or to have done.

44. What is a voter and a ballot?

The citizen who votes is called a voter or an elector, and the right of voting is called the suffrage. The voter puts on a piece of paper what he wishes. Such a piece of paper is called a ballot.

THE GIFT OF CITIZENSHIP IS FROM THE NATION, but the suffrage is conferred and regulated by the States.

45. Why is an education a necessity in a Republic?

In this country, where the people govern, it is of the highest importance, not only that the people should be intelligent, but that their intelligence should be educated. Ignorance is the most dangerous of enemies in a government of the people. If the people are without knowledge and are unable to avail themselves of the experience of the past, they can never govern either wisely or well; TO GOVERN OTHERS, THEREFORE, WE MUST FIRST LEARN TO GOVERN OURSELVES.

46. What is Public Education and the School of the People?

Out of this great necessity of learning how best to govern ourselves has gradually grown up in the United States a system of

PUBLIC EDUCATION. Each one of the forty-five States of the Union, as a matter of self-protection against the evil of ignorance, has undertaken to see that its people are duly prepared for AMERICAN CITIZENSHIP. To that end, therefore, there has been established by law in each State a system of public schools —THE SCHOOLS OF THE PEOPLE.

47. How can we learn to govern ourselves?

By helping the Public Schools in their work of teaching us how to GOVERN OURSELVES, so that in a few years we shall be fully prepared to earn an honest living and shall know how to help govern the people and how to help make the laws.

48. What is the aim of the Public School?

The public school aims to do two separate things for us:

First. To train us in such habits of behavior as will best fit us to become GOOD MEMBERS OF CIVIL SOCIETY and PATRIOTIC AMERICAN CITIZENS.

Second. To instruct us through the arts of reading and writing in the use of books, in order that we may gain and learn how best to use the knowledge which millions of wise men and women, who have lived in other times, under all sorts of conditions and in all parts of the world, have discovered and recorded for our use.

49. What must we do when training in behavior?

The first step in learning to govern ourselves is to learn how to obey—TO BE OBEDIENT TO GOVERNMENT.

50. What is the government of the family?

We came under a government when we were born; that government was the GOVERNMENT OF THE FAMILY. One of our first lessons at home is to obey the authority of our parents or guardian. We do this because very young children do not know what is best for them, and so for their own good they must be obedient to home rule. Our home, therefore, is the first school in which we learn to be little citizens; and so we see how necessary the right kind of a home is, if we wish to become good citizens.

51. What is the government of the school?

From our home we go to the school, and here we find a new kind of government, the GOVERNMENT OF THE SCHOOL. At the head of this government is our PRINCIPAL with TEACHERS to assist in governing.

Now what is this government for? For the good of one little pupil only, like the home school? No; but to secure the greatest good for all the pupils from many homes. We have seen that this great Republic in which we live is made up of citizens, a great many of whom have come from foreign lands. So, likewise, in this school, we find children whose parents came from many countries; sometimes as many as twelve different nations are represented in one school.

52. Why is the school called a little republic?

The school, as regards the children, IS A LITTLE AMERICAN REPUBLIC, made up of LITTLE CITIZENS. Here we find ourselves for the first time as one among many, and we are brought into public contact with other children of our own age, who have equal rights with ourselves. It is in this school that we are to be taught one of the great lessons of life—TO RESPECT THE RIGHTS AND OPINIONS OF OTHERS, no matter what may be our schoolmates' color, or race, or religion, or birthplace; no matter whether their parents have very little money, or a great deal of money, or what may be their occupation. We are all a part of the GREAT AMERICAN NATION, that stands for equal rights for all before the law.

53. What is the object of school laws and how are we to obey them?

The first thing, therefore, we little citizens of this school must do IS TO OBEY ITS RULES AND LAWS. The object of these rules and laws is to train us all in regularity, punctuality, self-restraint, industry, order and truthful accuracy in all our work, and this is the way we can best help our teachers and perfect ourselves in good behavior.

54. What is our duty to ourselves?

We must not miss a single day at school, and must be punctual every morning and every afternoon.

We must come to school with a clean face, clean hands and clean clothes. We must be neat in our person and in our dress.

We must be orderly, and have a place for everything, and we must try to keep everything in its place.

We must be very attentive to what we are studying or doing, and do it with all our might.

We must try to keep our temper always and never get into a passion, no matter how much we may be provoked.

We must always be cheerful and never lose our courage.

We must never be afraid to tell the WHOLE TRUTH.

Lastly, we must try to do right because it is right, and then we shall all learn how to respect ourselves.

55. What is our duty to our associates?

We must always obey and be respectful to our teachers, listening attentively when they are speaking, because they are older than we are, and know so much more than we do.

We must be kind and polite to all our schoolmates, always respecting their rights and never taking advantage of them because we are stronger or bigger than they are, or because we think we know more than they know. Only cowards oppress those weaker than themselves.

We must never wantonly hurt a dumb animal, but must treat all animals kindly.

Lastly, we must never forget that we are LITTLE AMERICAN CITIZENS; proud of our HOME, proud of our SCHOOL and proud of our COUNTRY.

And so we shall learn little by little, day by day, how to govern ourselves, and when we can do that and are grown up, we shall know something about governing other people, and how to help make laws for our country.

56. What do we now know?

We now know a little about what a representative government is, what a republic is, what a citizen is; that a citizen of one State enjoys all the rights of a citizen of the forty-five other States, because he is a citizen of the United States; what the ballot is and what voting is; that the Constitution of the United States is the supreme law of the land; how many, many years it took the colonists and the American Nation to firmly establish this government of the people, and how much treasure and how many thousand men's lives it has cost to establish, defend, preserve and maintain it.

57. What do we wish to know?

We wish to learn a great deal more about our rights and our duties, both as little American citizens and grown-up citizens, and about the machinery or method the people use to govern the village, or the town, or the city, and county and State in which we live, and how all these separate governments fit into and work smoothly with the government of the whole United States under the Constitution we have been talking about.

58. What must we learn?

All this and a great deal more we must learn in order that when we grow up we may be THE MOST INTELLIGENT, THE MOST LAW-RESPECTING AND THE MOST PATRIOTIC OF AMERICAN CITIZENS; but we have learned enough to understand that this great and prosperous country in which we are growing up is doing wonderful things for each one of us, although as yet we can do very little for it.

59. What does this government of ours do for us?

It protects us and our parents and friends day and night from harm of all kinds; it protects us all in the enjoyment of the rights of citizenship; it treats all alike, no matter what their color, their birthplace or their religion; it enables our parents to feed and shelter and clothe us, and it gives us friends to help us and to be kind to us.

60. Why do we respect this nation?

Because we feel a profound respect for these United States, and for the brave men who in the days of the Revolution dared to risk their lives and fortunes that America might be a free land, and that we who came after them might perpetuate and enjoy the blessings of liberty.

61. Why do we especially love Our Country?

We feel especially thankful, and LOVE OUR COUNTRY for giving us such opportunities for education, free from all cost to our parents; for giving us the privilege of coming to this pleasant school with its light, warm and cheerful rooms, filled with conveniences for teaching us; for giving us these kind and patient teachers to help us learn so much that we wish to know, and who have taught us the patriotic songs, the singing of which we enjoy so much.

62. How, then, can we best express our respect and love?

By giving to our country in return for all these benefits and gifts the best we have, and that is our heads and hearts. Our head is the seat of our mind and our intellect; our heart is the fountain of our affections and our love. These are our dearest possessions. God is love, and gives us all these blessings; therefore, it is right that we shall recognize first of all the Ruler of the universe, the Almighty God. Hence we give our heads and our hearts to God first, and our country a'terwards, so that we shall be brought very close to the Creator, and His Spirit shall abide with us day by day, and make us better and happier.

63. What is the symbol of Our Nation?

The symbol of the Nation is the NATIONAL FLAG, the STARS AND STRIPES. IT STANDS FOR OUR HOME, FOR OUR SCHOOL, FOR OUR COUNTRY. The honor of the Nation is the honor of its Flag, and thus we do honor to the Nation in honoring the Flag.

64. What do we mean by the salutation of the Flag?

The mark of respect among all nations is uncovering the head, the expression of love is to touch the heart. Hence we have been taught to say—as we touch, first our foreheads, and next our hearts—"WE GIVE OUR HEADS!—AND OUR HEARTS!—TO GOD! AND OUR COUNTRY!"

In a country where people from many nations are gathered together to enjoy the inestimable blessings which America offers, we little citizens think it right and just that the American principles, the American language and the American Flag SHOULD BE SUPREME OVER ALL OTHERS, and so we complete our salute with the words, "ONE COUNTRY!—ONE LANGUAGE!—ONE FLAG!"

65. What is this mark of respect called?

This mark of respect and love we feel for GOD, our Country and Flag, we call "The American Patriotic Salute," and the boys and girls who enlist under the banner and use the salute are loyal volunteers in the Grand Army of Patriotic Americans, marching shoulder to shoulder in the cause of our COUNTRY and FLAG.

66. How should we feel when we salute our Flag?

When we salute the flag we will remember that we do it by virtue of the free will of this school. When we rise in our places to perform this patriotic act we will shout joyfully, and will salute our country through its flag with our whole soul. Let us be proud of our country, and as we learn more about its wonderful history may we become more and more GRATEFUL TO GOD for all the inestimable privileges, rights and blessings which are ours to enjoy, and may we never, NEVER do an act unworthy of the proud title of A CITIZEN OF THE UNITED STATES OF AMERICA.

67. Where can we receive further information concerning the early history of our country and its government?

By reading carefully the story of our country's birth and progress, and by studying the "Declaration of Independence" and the "Constitution of the United States of America."

OUR FLAG.

1. What is the meaning of a flag?
That which flags or hangs down loosely; an ensign or colors; a banner, or standard on which are certain emblems.
2. What is our Flag?
It is the emblem of Liberty and Independence.
3. What does our Flag represent?
The United States of America.
4. By what name is it known?
Star Spangled Banner, Stars and Stripes, Old Glory and Red, White and Blue.
5. Can you describe the Flag?
It is composed of seven red and six white stripes with a number of stars on a blue field in the upper left-hand corner.
6. What is the object of a flag?
Principally to indicate nationality and citizenship.
7. What does a flag symbolize?
The declaration of the principles of the nation it represents.
8. Do all the nations have the same form of flag?
No. Each nation has its own peculiar design, colors and emblem.
9. Is the use of flags of early or recent origin?
Of early origin. Ensigns, banners and standards are frequently mentioned in the Bible to distinguish one tribe from another.
10. When was the first legislative action taken for the establishment of an American flag?
January 2, 1776.

11. What was the design?

It had the "King's colors" as a union, and the body of the flag was composed of thirteen stripes, alternate red and white, to represent the colonies.

12. When was the first recorded "legislative action" taken for the adoption of the Stars and Stripes?

In a resolution offered by the Continental Congress at Philadelphia, Pa., June 14, 1777.

13. What was the resolution?

"Resolved, That the flag of the thirteen United States be thirteen stripes, alternate red and white; that the Union be thirteen stars, white in a blue field, representing a new constellation."

14. Who were the members of the committee appointed by Congress to design a national flag?

General Washington, Col. George Ross and Robert Morris.

15. Who made the first flag combining the stars and stripes?

Mrs. Betsey Ross at her residence, 239 Arch street, Philadelphia, Pa.

16. Under whose direction was the flag made?

Under the personal supervision and direction of General Washington, between May 23 and June 7, 1777.

17. To whom does the credit of designing the Stars and Stripes belong?

Undoubtedly to General Washington. Both Stars and Stripes were suggested by the arms and crest of his ancestors, which contain both stripes and five pointed stars.

18. What was the material used in the first Stars and Stripes?

A soldier's white shirt, an old blue army overcoat and a red flannel petticoat.

19. How long did the Stars and Stripes remain unchanged after their adoption in 1777?

About eighteen years, until January 15, 1794, when Congress enacted, "That from and after the first day of May, 1795, the flag of the United States be fifteen stripes, alternate red and white; that the union be fifteen stars, white in a blue field."

20. Why did Congress make this change in the flag?

On account of new States being admitted into the Union.

21. How long did this flag remain unchanged?

From May 1, 1795, to March 24, 1818, during which period occurred the War of 1812 with Great Britain.

22. Why was the flag changed again?

Because when new States were admitted into the Union the flag became too wide.

23. By what legislative act did Congress restore the flag to its original design?

"Section 1. Be it enacted that from and after the fourth day of July next the flag of the United States be thirteen horizontal stripes, alternate red and white; that the union have twenty stars, white in a blue field."

"Section 2. And be it further enacted that on the admission of every new State into the Union one star be added to the union of the flag, and that such addition shall take effect on the fourth day of July next succeeding such admission."

24. To whom does the credit of restoring the Stars and Stripes to its original design belong?

Captain Samuel Chester Reid, United States Navy, who retained the thirteen original stripes, but added a star for every new State admitted to the Union.

25. Have there been any further changes in our flag since 1818?

No. It is the same to-day as it was when originally adopted on June 14, 1777, except as to the number and arrangement of the stars.

26. What is meant by the field or union in the flag?

It is the blue that contains the white stars.

27. How many stars are there in the union of the flag up to the present time?

Forty-five, or one for each admitted State.

28. How are the stars arranged in the union?

In horizontal parallel rows across the blue field.

29. What do the stars symbolize?

The perpetuity of the Union. "In union there is strength." "United we stand, divided we fall."

30. How many stripes in our flag?

Thirteen, alternate red and white.

31. What do they represent?

The thirteen original States of the Union.

32. What does the red signify?

Divine love; valor; war. The color calls to mind the blood shed for our country.

33. What does the white express?

Truth, hope, purity and peace.

34. What does the blue denote?

Loyalty, sincerity and justice.

35. What are the United States regulations for the dimensions of the Stars and Stripes?

The material must be all-wool American bunting, or silk. The union must be one-third the length of the flag, extending to the botton of the fourth red stripe.

36. When and where was the first American Flag unfurled?

It was first raised over Fort Stanivix, on the present site of the city of Rome, N. Y., August 2, 1777.

37. Who first raised the Stars and Stripes on a vessel at sea and took them to a foreign country?

Captain John Paul Jones, commander of the "Ranger," which arrived at the port of France, December 1, 1777.

38. When was the first salute given the American Flag by a foreign country?

On February 14, 1778, at a French port by foreign naval vessels.

39. When did our flag take its first trip around the world?

September 30, 1787, and was three years in girding the globe.

40. What is the national salute to the flag?

One gun for each State admitted to the Union, fired at noon on July 4, by military and naval stations provided with artillery.

41. What is the salute of our national flag?

Twenty-one guns.

42. How do the officers and men of the United States army and navy salute the flag?

By raising the extended right hand to the forehead, palm downward.

43. How many different designs of flags in this country were made before the Stars and Stripes were adopted?

From 1494 to the present time there were sixty-four (64) different designs.

44. What should we all do on passing the schoolhouse flag or in a military camp, or on boarding a United States war vessel?

Uncover and bow the head. It will be appreciated, and you will be honoring the flag of your country.

45. How old is our flag?

One hundred and twenty years. Although our COUNTRY is the youngest of the great nations of the world, its FLAG is the oldest.

46. When was the first flag made in the United States from American manufactured bunting?

It was made February 21, 1866, and was displayed February 24, 1866, over the United States Senate Chamber at Washington, D. C.

47. When the flag is hoisted at half-mast, what does it mean?

It is a mark of mourning for one of our distinguished citizens.

48. When the flag is raised with the union down, what does it mean?

It means disgrace or is a signal of distress.

49. What does our flag mean for its citizens?

It means FREE SPEECH, FREE SCHOOLS and FREE THOUGHT.

ORIGIN AND HISTORY

OF OUR

NATIONAL HYMNS AND PATRIOTIC SONGS.

Our national hymns and songs have been a power in electrifying the heart of the American patriot, and are now inspiring millions of little citizens in the public schools of our native land with tender emotions for their country and flag.

THE AMERICAN FLAG.

The author of this soul-inspiring song and poem, Joseph Rodman Drake, was born in New York, August 7, 1795, and died September 21, 1820.

The "American Flag" was written between the 20th and 25th days of May, 1819, when the author was not quite twenty-four, and originally concluded with the following lines:

> "As fixed as yonder orb divine
> That saw the bannered blaze unfurled,
> Shall thy proud stars resplendent shine,
> The guard and glory of the world."

These lines not being satisfactory to Mr. Drake, he consulted his friend, Fitz Green Halleck, to suggest a better stanza. Mr. Halleck, in a glowing burst of patriotism, sat down and wrote the four concluding lines, which are as follows:

> "Forever float that standard sheet!
> Where breathes the foe but falls before us,
> With Freedom's soil beneath our feet,
> And Freedom's banner streaming o'er us."

The poem, from the beginning to the conclusion, breathes a pure patriotism that is from the heart, inspired by the love of country, and awakens the tenderest emotions of the soul and body of every one who reads it.

THE AMERICAN FLAG.

Joseph Rodman Drake.   Music by Bellini.

When Freedom from her mountain height
  Unfurled her standard to the air,
She tore the azure robe of night,
  And set the stars of glory there!
She mingles with its gorgeous dyes
The milky baldrick of the skies.
And striped its pure celestial white
With streakings of the morning light.
Then, from her mansion in the sun,
  She called her eagle bearer down,
And gave into his mighty hand
The symbol of her chosen land.

Majestic monarch of the cloud!
  Who rear'st aloft thy regal form,
To hear the tempest trumping loud,
And see the lightning lances driven,
When strive the warriors of the storm,
  And rolls the thunder-drum of heaven!
Child of the sun! to thee 'tis given
  To guard the banner of the free!
To hover in the sulphur smoke,
To ward away the battle stroke,
And bid its blendings shine afar,
Like rainbows on the clouds of war.

Flag of the brave! thy folds shall fly,
  The sign of hope and triumph high!
When speaks the signal trumpet tone,
And the long line comes gleaming on;
Ere the life-blood, warm and wet,
Has dimm'd the glist'ning bayonet—
Each soldier eye shall brightly turn
To where thy sky-born glories burn.
Flag of the free heart's hope and home,
  By angel hands to valor given!
Thy stars have lit the welkin dome,
  And all thy hues were born in heaven.

Flag of the seas! on ocean's wave
Thy stars shall glitter o'er the brave,
When death, careering on the gale.
Sweeps darkly round the bellied sail,
And frighted waves rush wildly back
Before the broadside's reeling rack;
The dying wanderer of the sea
Shall look at once to heav'n and thee.
Forever float that standard sheet!
  Where breathes the foe but falls before us,
With Freedom's soil beneath our feet.
  And Feedom's banner streaming o'er us.

AMERICA.

My Country 'Tis of Thee.

The author, Rev. S. F. Smith, was born in Boston, Mass., October 21, 1808, and was an honored member of the Baptist denomination, residing at Newton Centre, Mass. He died November 16, 1895. Dr. Smith was graduated from Harvard in the famous class of 1829, with Oliver Wendel Holmes, and from Andover Theological Seminary in 1832, entering the ministry in 1834.

"America" was written while he was a student at Andover. The melody is that of a German hymn in a collection which Dr. Lowell Mason brought to him for translation. Turning over the leaves of the book, one gloomy day in February, 1832, he came across the air—"God Save the King." He liked the music, and glanced at the German words at the foot of the page, and under the inspiration of the moment took up his pen and in half an hour the grand old hymn was born. The young student had no idea at the time how much he had done for his country.

The hymn was first used at a children's Fourth of July celebration at Park Church, Boston, and the results were surprising. The fervent lines leaped like wild fire from lip to lip, and from heart to heart all over our blessed land, filling the soul with loyalty to God and our country. It has been sung in every country in the world, and from the highest peak above the clouds in the Rocky Mountains. It was an inspiration to the soldiers both North and South during the War of the Rebellion, and stimulated them on the march, in camp and in the hospital. Its words have been chanted from the decks of our ships and war vessels under the Stars and Stripes. It has been sung by more than 18,000,000 children in our Sunday and Public schools. It breathes a pure love for God and our country and fills the soul with intense love and patriotism.

AMERICA—My Country 'Tis of Thee.

My coun-try, 'tis of thee Sweet land of lib-er-ty,
My na-tive coun-try, thee—Land of the no-ble, free-

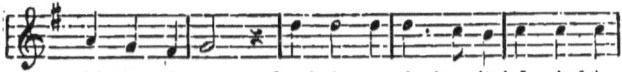

Of thee I sing; Land where my fa-thers died, Land of the
Thy name I love; I love thy rocks and rills, Thy woods and

pilgrim's pride, From ev-'ry mountain side Let free-dom ring.
templed hills My heart with rapture thrills Like that a-bove.

Let music swell the breeze,
And ring from all the trees,
  Sweet freedom's song.
Let mortal tongues awake;
Let all that breathe partake;
Let rocks their silence break;
  The sound prolong.

Our father's God, to Thee,
Author of liberty,
  To Thee we sing:
Long may our land be bright
With freedom's holy light;
Protect us by thy might,
  Great God our King.

PATRIOTISM IN YOUTH.

A group of seventeen young girls, with their teacher, on the day before Memorial Day, were making button-hole bouquets for the veterans in a Western city. Rev. S. F. Smith, D. D., author of "My Country 'Tis of Thee," was present, and while they intermingled patriotic songs with their graceful labors, wrote the following description of the scene:

Sweet in the innocence of youth,
  Born of the brave and free,
They wove fair garlands while they sang
  "My Country 'Tis of Thee,"
How every bosom swelled with joy,
  And thrilled with grateful pride,
As, fond their whispering cadence breath'd
  "Land where my fathers died."

Fair flowers in sweet bouquets they tied,
  Breaths from the vales and hills,
While childish voices poured the strain,
  "I love thy rocks and rills,"
Each face grew radiant with the thought
  "Land of the noble free."
Each voice seemed reverent as it trilled
  "Sweet land of liberty."

And bud and bloom, and leaf they bound,
  And bade the living keep
Unharmed and pure the cherished graves
  Where brave men calmly sleep:
And thus while infant lips begin
  To lisp "Sweet freedom's song,"
Manhood's deep tones from age to age,
  Shall still "The sound prolong."

I hailed the promise of the scene,
  Gladness was in the strain;
The glorious land is safe while love
  Still swells the glad refrain:
And what shall be our sure defense?
  Who guards our liberty?
Not men, not arms alone—we look
  "Our father's God, to Thee."

THE STAR SPANGLED BANNER.

The author of this soul inspiring lyric, Francis Scott Key, was born August 9, 1780, at Terra Rubra, near Double Pipe Creek, Carroll County, Md., and died in Baltimore, January 11, 1843. His remains were removed September, 1866, to Frederick, Md., and reinterred in Mt. Olivet Cemetery.

Francis Scott Key was a lawyer by profession, and the song, which has immortalized his name and become national, was inspired by him while a prisoner on board of the Cartel Ship Minden, witnessing the bombardment of Fort McHenry, Md., by the British, between midnight and dawn September 13, 1814. The scene which he described made his heart sick with anxiety; the warm patriotism breathed in the song was not the offspring of fancy or mere sentiment or poetic imagination. He describes what he actually saw in the dim light of that September morning, and tells us how he felt when he could not see the flag through the smoke of battle, and what his feelings were when the battle was over, and the victory was won by his countrymen. Every word came warm from the depths of his throbbing heart and filled his soul with thankfulness to the Divine hand that turned the tide of battle for Liberty.

The song was first published September 21, 1814, in the "Baltimore American," and was first sung in a tavern adjoining the Haliday Street Theatre, by Charles Durang, and then in the theatre, where it took the popular fancy until the entire audience seemed inspired by its pathetic eloquence. The song has filled the hearts of citizens and soldiers alike with intense enthusiasm and never fails to find a patriotic response in the hearts of those who listen to the glorious hymn.

STAR SPANGLED BANNER.

1. O say, can you see by the dawn's early light, What so proudly we hail'd at the
2. On the shore dimly seen thro' the mists of the deep, Where the foe's haughty host in dread
3. And where is that band who so vauntingly swore That the havoc of war and the
4. Oh, thus be it ever when Freemen shall stand Between their lov'd homes and the

twilight's last gleaming? Whose broad stripes and bright stars thro' the perilous fight, On the
si-lence re-pos-es ; What is that which the breeze, o'er the towering steep? As it
bat-tle's con-fus-ion A home and a country shall leave us no more— Their
war's desolation; Blest with vict'ry and peace, may the Heav'n rescu'd land, Praise the

ramparts we watch'd were so gallantly streaming; And the rocket's red glare, the bombs
fit-ful-ly blows, half conceals, half discloses? Now it catch-es the gleam of the
blood has wash'd out their foul footsteps' pollution, No ref-uge could save the
pow'r that hath made and preserv'd us a nation. Then conquer we must, when our

bursting in air, Gave proof thro' the night that our Flag was still there. O say, does that
morning's first beam, In full glory reflect'd, now shines in the stream, 'Tis the Star Spangl'd
hireling and slave From the terror of death, or the gloom of the grave; And the Star Spangl'd
cause it is just, And this be our motto : "In God is our trust." And the Star Spangl'd

Star Spangled Banner yet wave, O'er the Land of the Free, and the home of the Brave.
Banner! Oh! long may it wave, O'er the Land of the Free, and the home of the Brave.
Banner, in triumph shall wave, O'er the Land of the Free, and the home of the Brave.
Banner, in triumph doth wave, O'er the Land of the Free, and the home of the Brave.

COLUMBIA, THE GEM OF THE OCEAN.
Sometimes called the "Red, White and Blue."

This hymn is known as the army and navy song, because it is adapted to reunions of the two services. The original song was written and composed by David T. Shaw, an actor, under the title "Columbia, the Land of the Brave," and was published in 1843. Though the name and idea seem to have originated with Shaw, an American, the words and music, as printed and sung, are conceded to Thomas A. Beckett, an Englishman, in which it was known by the first name above.

The hymn was sung for the first time in the fall of 1843 at the Chestnut Street Theatre, Philadelphia, Pa.

Written and Composed by DAVID T. SHAW.

1. O Columbia! the gem of the ocean, The home of the brave and the free, The shrine of each patriot's devotion, A world offers homage to thee. Thy mandates make heroes as-semble, When Li-ber-ty's form stands in view, Th.. banners make ty-ran-ny tremble, When borne by the red, white and blue, When borne by the red, white and blue, When borne by the red, white and blue, Thy banners make tyranny tremble, When borne by the red, white and blue.

2. When war winged its wide desolation, And threatened the land to de-form, The ark then of freedom's foundation, Columbia, rode safe through the storm; With her garlands of vict'ry a-round her, When so proudly she bore her brave crew, With her flag proudly float-ing before her, The boast of the red, white and blue, The boast of the red, white and blue, The boast of the red, white and blue, With her flag proudly floating before her, The boast of the red, white and blue.

HAIL, COLUMBIA.

The author of "Hail, Columbia" was the Hon. Joseph Hopkinson, LL. D., Vice-President of the American Philosophical Society, and President of the Pennsylvania Academy of Fine Arts, etc.

Mr. Hopkinson wrote the song April, 1798, at his residence, 132 Spruce Street, Philadelphia, Pa., when he was twenty-eight years old. He died in Philadelphia, January 15, 1842.

The object of Mr. Hopkinson, in writing the song, was to unite two parties in our country. It was at a time when war with France was thought to be inevitable. The contest between England and France was raging, and the people of the United States were divided in their opinions. To counteract any feeling for either England or France, he aimed to arouse an American spirit, which should be independent of, and above the interests, passion and policy of both belligerents, and look and feel exclusively for our honor and rights.

No illusion is made to France or England or the quarrel between them, or to the question which was most in fault in their treatment of us.

The song was called for on Saturday, completed on Sunday, and sung for the first time on Monday evening at the theatre. It was encored and repeated eight times, the audience, at last, joining in the chorus. The song had the desired effect in uniting both factions, and was received with great favor and enthusiasm by Americans everywhere.

(Words and Music on next page.)

HAIL COLUMBIA.

1. Hail! Co-lum-bia, happy land! Hail! ye heroes, heav'n born band,
2. Immortal patriots, rise once more, Defend your rights, defend your shore;

Who fought and bled in freedom's cause, Who fought and bled in
Let no rude foe with im-pi-ous hand, Let no rude foe with

free-dom's cause, And when the storm of war was gone,
im-pi-ous hand In-vade the shrine where sa-cred lies

En-joyed the peace your val-or won. Let In-de-pend-ence
Of toil and blood the well earn'd price; While offering peace

be our boast, Ev-er mind-ful what it cost,
sincere and just, In heav'n we place a man-ly trust,

Ev-er grateful for the price, Let its al-tar reach the skies.
That truth and justice may prevail, And ev-'ry scheme of bondage fail.

CHORUS.

Firm, u-nit-ed let us be, Ral-ly-ing round our Lib-er-ty,

As a band of brothers join'd, Peace and safety we shall find.

THE BATTLE HYMN OF THE REPUBLIC.

The author of this stirring lyric, Julia Ward, daughter of Samuel Ward, Esq., was born in New York, May 27th, 1819, and married to Dr. S. G. Howe in 1843.

The Battle Hymn of the Republic was written in Washington under the following circumstances : Mrs. Howe, with a party of friends, had gone out some distance from the city to witness a military review, and were surprised by a Confederate raid, and for some moments the wildest excitement prevailed, as it was feared their retreat would be cut off. When at last the carriage containing the party of spectators was turned towards Washington, it was driven very slowly, with an armed escort on either side, while the ladies sung "John Brown's Body," in brave defiance of their late alarm.

The grand, ringing tune deserved noble words and inspired Mrs. Howe to wish that she might write them. She was so impressed with the song on retiring for the night that her wish must have followed her in her dreams. She awoke in the gray dawn of the morning with the verses spinning themselves in her mind. Fearing to lose them, should she fall asleep again, she arose, and in the uncertain morning twilight scribbled them off, not looking at the paper under her hand. She returned to bed and fell asleep, unconscious that the almost illegible scrawl was the one grand hymn of the war, and has placed her name among the best of our patriotic writers.

(Words and Music on next page.)

BATTLE HYMN OF THE REPUBLIC.

JULIA WARD HOWE.   Air: "John Brown's Body."

1. Mine eyes have seen the glo-ry of the com-ing of the Lord; He is
2. I have seen Him in the watchfires of a hundred circling camps; They have
3. He has sounded forth the trumpet that shall never call re-treat; He is
4. In the beau-ty of the lil-ies, Christ was born across the sea, With a

trampling out the vintage where the grapes of wrath are stored; He hath loosed the
build-ed Him an al-tar in the evening dews and damps; I can read His
sift-ing out the hearts of men be-fore His judgment seat; Oh, be swift, my
glo-ry in His bo-som that trans-fig-ures you and me; As He died to

fate-ful lightning of His ter-ri-ble swift sword, His truth is marching on.
righteous sentence by the dim and flar-ing lamps, His day is marching on.
soul, to answer Him! be ju-bi-lant, my feet, Our God is marching on.
make men ho-ly, let us die to make men free, While God is marching on.

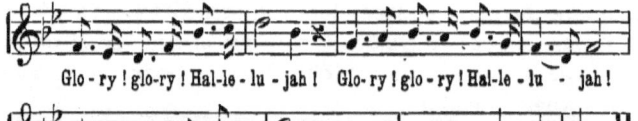

Glo-ry! glo-ry! Hal-le-lu-jah! Glo-ry! glo-ry! Hal-le-lu-jah!

Glo-ry! glo-ry! Hal-le-lu-jah! His truth is march-ing on.

YANKEE DOODLE.

Rear-Admiral Preble, U. S. N., in his most excellent work, "History of our Flag," says:

"The introduction of the song to Americans has been ascribed to Dr. Shuchburg, a surgeon of the regular troops in Albany, N. Y., about 1737. The common account of the origin of 'Yankee Doodle,' which ascribes it to Dr. Shuchburg, was written by Nathan H. Carter, and published in the 'Albany Statesman,' nearly three-fourths of a century after the event is said to have happened."

The time-honored song seems to be a musical vagabond and is wrapped in obscurity, a literary Bohemian. The words are older than our Revolution and originated in the time of Charles II.

While Yankee Doodle is National property, it is not a literary treasure of the highest value, however no true born Yankee is ashamed of the song.

> 'Twill do to whistle, sing or play,
> And is just the tune for fighting.

Our American ancestors revived the expression, history has emphasized it. Its spirit and sentiment have come down to us through many ages to be embodied in American laws, institutions and character. It keeps alive the memories of the good old Continental days, and is patriotic music for the present generation and will be for the next and next.

YANKEE DOODLE.

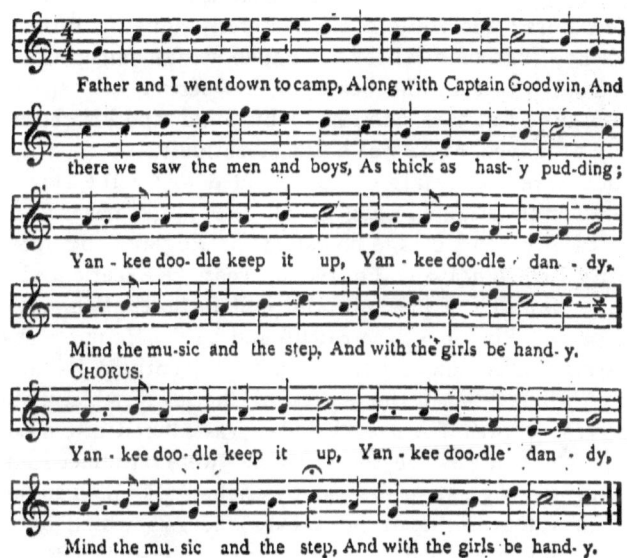

And there was General Washington,
  Upon a snow white charger,
He look'd as big as all out doors,
  Some thought he was much larger.

And there they had a copper gun,
  Big as a log of maple,
They tied it to a wooden cart,
  A load for Father's cattle.

And there I see'd a little keg,
  All bound around with leather,
They beat it with two little sticks,
  To call the men together.

But I can't tell you half I see'd,
  They kept up such a smother,
I took my hat off, made a bow,
  And scamper'd home to Mother

HOME, SWEET HOME.

The author of "Home, Sweet Home," John Howard Payne, was born in New York City, June 9, 1792, and died at Tunis, April 10, 1852.

John Howard was a leader among the boys in sports and lessons, too. He raised a little military company which he once marched to general training, where Major-General Elliott extended a formal invitation to the gallant young captain, who led his troops into the ranks to be reviewed with the veterans of the Revolution.

At the age of thirteen he became a clerk in a mercantile house in New York; and while a clerk secretly edited a little paper called the "Thespian Mirror." Payne was an engaging youth, he won all hearts by the beauty of his person, his captivating address, the premature richness of his mind, and his chaste and flowing utterance, as he was a fine elocutionist.

When seventeen years old he decided to try the stage, and achieved wonderful success in all the large Eastern cities. When twenty years of age he sailed for England and appeared in Drury Lane Theatre. For twenty years he experienced more than the mingling of pleasure and evil fortune. While he was much praised his life was sorrowful and hard. He wrote several successful dramas, among them was a play entitled "Clari, the Maid of Milan," but at the request of Charles Kemble, manager of Convent Garden Theatre, the play was altered into an opera and the words of "Home, Sweet Home" were introduced into it. The song was a great success and enriched all who handled it, while the author did not receive even the £25 which he reckoned as his share when the manuscript was sold. Payne returned to America in 1832, and nine years later received the appointment of American Consul at Tunis.

In his own words he lamented his life, when he says: "How often while in the large cities of foreign countries have I heard persons singing "Home, Sweet Home," without having a shilling to buy myself the next meal or a place to lay my head." "The world has literally sung my song until every heart is familiar with its melody, yet I have been a wanderer from my boyhood."

With due consideration for the sorrows of his career he forsook his home and associations and voluntarily attached himself to a class of adventurers who lived by their wits. His life most certainly was a pathetic one, and his song has brought the tears to the eyes of many a poor wanderer in a foreign land. May the history and song of the author bring sweet contentment to every boy and girl who reads or sings the lines.

'Mid pleasures and palaces though we may roam,
Be it ever so humble, there's no place like home;
A charm from the skies seems to hallow us there,
Which seek thro' the world is ne'er met with elsewhere.

Chorus—

Home, home, sweet, sweet home,
There's no place like home, there's no place like home.

I gaze on the moon as I tread the drear wild,
And feel that my mother now thinks of her child,
As she looks on that moon from her own cottage door,
Thro' the wood-bine whose fragrance shall cheer me no more.

An exile from home, splendor dazzles in vain;
Oh, give me my lowly thatch'd cottage again;
The birds singing gaily, that came at my call;
Give me them, and that peace of mind, dearer than all.

SALUTE OLD GLORY.

By Kate Brownlee Sherwood.

This song is dedicated to the 10,000,000 little American citizens who are saluting the flag as part of their school exercises and who are invited to join in the Patriotic work for inetlligent citizenship. It may be sung to the tune of "Dixie."

Hail, fairest flag on land or ocean,
Setting all the world in motion!
 Awake! awake!
 Salute the flag!
Its stars so bright, its stripes so fair;
 Awake! awake!
No other can with it compare,
That sails the sea, that rules the air;
 Awake! awake!
 Awake! salute Old Glory!

(Continued on next page.)

SALUTE OLD GLORY—Continued.

Our flag has felt the tempest's rattle,
Blown by all the winds of battle.
    Awake! awake!
    Salute the flag!
For you its beauteous folds were torn;
    Awake! awake!
But now by loyal legions borne,
It vies the splendors of the morn;
    Awake! awake!
    Awake! salute Old Glory!

O come, ye patriots, to the rally!
Come from every hill and valley!
    Awake! awake!
    Salute the flag!
The Stars and Stripes for freedom stand;
    Awake! awake!
O come, and for your country band,
And pledge your head and heart and hand,
    Awake! awake!
    Awake! salute Old Glory!

KELLER'S AMERICAN HYMN.

Speed our Republic, O Father on high;
  Lead us in pathways of justice and right;
Rulers as well as the ruled, "One and all,"
  Girdle with virtue the armor of night.

Hail, three times hail, to our country and flag!
  (Repeat last two lines as chorus.)

Foremost in battle for freedom we stand,
  We rush to arms when aroused by its call;
Still, as of yore, when George Washington led,
  Thunders our war-cry, "We conquer or fall."

Faithful and honest to friend and to foe,
  Willing to die in humanity's cause,
Thus we defy all tyrannical power,
  While we contend for our Union and laws.

Rise up, proud eagle, rise up to the clouds;
  Spread thy broad wings o'er this fair western world;
Fling from thy beak our dear banner of old,
  Show that it still is for freedom unfurled.

Hail, three times hail, to our country and flag!
  Rulers as well as ruled, "One and all,"
Girdle with virtue, the armor of night.
  Hail, three times hail, to our country and flag!

WASHINGTON'S PATRIOTISM

AND

LOVE FOR HIS COUNTRYMEN.

WALLACE FOSTER.

The name of Washington is familiar to every boy and girl in our country. His fame is widespread, and he is known as "*the father of our country.*" There was in the breast of Washington one sentiment so deeply felt, so constantly uppermost, that no proper occasion escaped without its utterance. In his "Farewell Address to the People of the United States," the Union was the great object of his thoughts. In this admirable bequest, like a true teacher sent from God, he dwells chiefly on our Union and brotherly love, in which he had the consolation to believe that, while choice and prudence invited him to quit the political scene, patriotism did not forbid it.

In looking forward to the moment in which he was to terminate his career in public life, his feelings did not permit him to suspend the deep acknowledgment of that debt of gratitude which he owed to his beloved country, for the many honors it had conferred upon him, and for the steadfast confidence with which it had supported him. He also had the satisfaction of knowing in his retirement that the involuntary errors he had probably committed had been the source of no serious or lasting mischief to his country; therefore, he expected to realize without alloy, the sweet enjoyment of partaking, in the midst of his fellow-citizens, the benign influence of good laws under a free government, the ever favorite object of his heart, and the happy reward for sharing the mutual cares, dangers and labors of his countrymen.

The birth of true religion appeared to him the one thing needful in the spring of political life. On this topic he employed all the energies of his mind; and in words worthy to be written in letters of gold, emphatically besought his countrymen to guard with holiest care "the unity of the government," as the main pillar and palladium of their liberty, their independence, and everything most dear to them on earth.

The constancy of the support of the people was the essential prop of his efforts and guaranteed to him the plans that were effected.

Profoundly impressed with the necessity of the people's continued faithfulness to their vows, he appealed that heaven might continue to distribute the choicest tokens of its beneficence to the people, that union and brotherly affection might be perpetual ; that the free constitution might be sacredly maintained ; that its administration in every department might be stamped with wisdom and virtue ; that, in fine, the happiness of the people in the thirteen States, under the auspices of liberty, might be made complete, by so careful a preservation and so prudent a use of this blessing, as will acquire to them the glory of recommending it to the applause, the affection and adoption of every nation which is yet a stranger to it.

Love of liberty was interwoven into every fiber of his heart; no recommendation is necessary to fortify or confirm the attachment.

The unity of government, which we now enjoy, was dear to Washington, and justly so, for it was the main pillar in the edifice of the real independence of the people; their support and tranquillity at home; their peace abroad; their safety and prosperity ; that very liberty which they so highly prized.

Washington's great love for the people of his country made him zealous for their collective and individual happiness—entreating them to cherish a cordial, habitual and immovable attachment for each other, accustom themselves to think and speak of their love of country as of the palladium of their political safety and prosperity ; to watch for its preservation with jealous anxiety; to discountenance whatever may suggest even a suspicion that it can, in any event, be abandoned, and indignantly, to frown upon the first dawning of every attempt to alienate any portion of their country from the rest, or to enfeeble the sacred ties which now link together that which they should accustom themselves to reverence.

The name of America inspired the father of our country with pride and kindled in his warm heart an unquenchable fire of patriotism, illuminating his soul with "malice toward none, and charity for all."

Washington was of the same noble spirit as the British Admiral Blake, one of the bravest and best patriots in the English navy, who, with all his dislike for Oliver Cromwell, fought gallantly under him, and with his dying breath exhorted his men "to love their country as a common mother, and no matter what hands the government might fall into to fight for her like good children." So Washington was often called to obey men greatly his inferiors, and to execute orders which he entirely disapproved, but he was never known to falter. Sensible of the infinite importance of union and order to the good of his country, he ever yielded a prompt obedience to her will, and not content with setting us through life so fair an example, he leaves us at his death this blessed advice: "Your government claims your utmost confidence and support. Respect for *its authority*, compliance with its laws, acquiescence in its measures, are duties enjoined by the fundamental maxims of true liberty. The basis of our political system is the right of the people to make and alter their constitutions of government. But the Constitution, which at any time exists until changed by an explicit and authentic act of the whole people, is sacredly obligatory upon all."

> A life how useful to his country led!
> How loved while living! how revered, now dead!
> Lisp! lisp his name, ye children yet unborn,
> And with like deeds your own great name adorn.

OUR CHIEFTAIN, WASHINGTON.

He knelt where Heaven's delicious breath
   Perfumed the woods with crimson leaf,
Here Washington, God's throne besieged
   To bring his countrymen relief.
Deep anguish like a whirlwind swept
   Our noble chieftain's heart with care,
Till quietly away he steals
   And whispers to his God in prayer.

The guns boom loud—the smoke ascends,
   But through it all Jehovah sees
That bending form, that pale young brow,
   Pleading beneath the hickory trees.
Oh, suffering, struggling leader, thou
   Hast won sweet mercy from the skies,
Cheer up, brave heart, the clouds dispel,
   It is no mirage that thine eyes

See through the cannonaded air,
   But the dear stars and glorious stripes
That float in signal triumph there.
   Hark! hear him tell those boys in blue,
Amid the drops of crimson rain,
   "Whene'er you feel like faltering—go
And pray, for Heaven will sustain."

—[A. E. Thomas.

GEN. WASHINGTON'S GENERAL ORDER, AUG. 3, 1776.

"That the troops may have an opportunity of attending public worship, as well as to take some rest after the great fatigue they have gone through, the General, in future, excuses them from fatigue duty on Sundays, except at the shipyards, or on special occasions, until further orders. The General is sorry to be informed that the foolish and wicked practice of profane cursing and swearing, a vice hitherto little known in an American army, is growing into fashion. He hopes the officers will, by example as well as influence, endeavor to check it, and that both they and the men will reflect that we can have little hope of the blessing of heaven on our arms, if we insult it by our impiety and folly. Added to this, it is a vice so mean and low, without any temptation, that every man of sense and character detests and despises it."

GOLDEN SENTIMENTS TO THE MEMORY OF WASHINGTON FROM THE SONS AND DAUGHTERS OF PATRIOTS.

Washington fought not for fame, but for liberty. Let his name be perpetuated and each recurring birthday anniversary celebrated.—Jane C Harvey, Minn.

"First in peace, first in war, and first in the hearts of his countrymen," was appropriately said of him. He rose above partisanship. He knew no section, party or creed.—T. E. Hickman, Ark.

Washington was the brightest type of American manhood that any nation has produced; his deeds are a monument to a well-spent life, and his work for his country will never die.—Ann M. Kocher, Penn.

O, immortal Washington! Thou greatest of America's uncrowned kings. in the unselfishness of thy love of home and native land, we would approach within the halo of thy greatness, and adorn thy brow with the laurel.—Robt. M. Smith, Ill.

Let all true American boys and girls resolve on the anniversary of Washington's birthday, that they will imitate in their own life, as far as lies within their power, the pre-eminent patriotism of the "Father of his country."—Burt Stone, Ia.

Well does February 22d deserve a place among our national holidays; it recalls to us the bright name on history's page, that of Washington, who fought for our independence, established our government, and secured the blessings of liberty to ourselves and our posterity.—Lillian Knight, Minn.

To Washington more than any other we owe the existence of our glorious Union. It was he who steered the newly-constructed Ship of State through the raging sea of disordered finance, prostrated commerce, ruined credit and exhausted resources into the placid waters that have brought us to our present greatness. What emotions of gratitude swell our hearts when we mention that significant synonym of our free institutions—Washington.—John E. Haslacker, West Va.

Washington was greater than all other men, simply because he was always true to himself and his duty. We can all do this if we only will. Let us begin now on the opening of our school, and never give up till the victory is won. It is in this that all "progress and patriotism" lies. Let us remember with pride that Washington was an American and we are Americans. We must do our very best, as he did. Then, and only then, shall we have nothing to fear in the morning and nothing to regret at night. That is to live and be free.—Christian Simenson, Minn.

We see unfurled proudly to the breeze, from the school-houses, from the public and private buildings of city and hamlet, the stars and stripes, emblem of a free and independent country, liberated from the oppressive rule of British sovereignty by the valor and discretion of Washington. May we fully realize the benefits of a government of the people, for the people and by the people, and pay a glowing tribute of respect to the nation, by celebrating the day that gave birth to the Father of our Country.—Henry J. Buchen, Wis.

GENERAL MARQUIS DE LAFAYETTE AND HIS LOVE FOR AMERICA.

H. D. ESTABROOK.

France, I salute you! In the name of Lafayette, whom you sent to us; in the name of Washington, whom we return to you, America joins with you, O sister of liberty, in that shout which yet shall engirdle the earth—"The king is dead; long live the republic!"

My countrymen, I have preached my sermon in advance. I propose to illustrate it by the life work of one man; not a genius, but a sane man, as Washington was sane; a good man, as Washington was good; a man who, born to every extrinsic advantage for which we worldings moil—title, riches, social caste—flung all his birthrights to the winds, and then reconquered from the world the homage of mankind, and from heaven the approval of Jehovah.

History has enshrined him; humanity may not forget him. France calls him father. Surely America, in whose name and for whose sake he yielded the title of "noble" for that of "man," bartered the coronet of a marquis for the toga of a citizen, giving to the word "citizen," indeed, a significance and glory. America, whose Washington clasped him to his heart of hearts, and called him son—surely, my countrymen, America will recall them thus forever joined—Washington and Lafayette.

LINCOLN'S ADDRESS AT GETTYSBURG.

President Lincoln's address when, the National Cemetery at Gettysburg, Pa., was dedicated November 19, 1863, was in these memorable words:

"Fourscore and seven years ago, our fathers brought forth upon this continent a new Nation, conceived in Liberty, and dedicated to the proposition that all men are created equal.

"Now we are engaged in a great Civil war, testing whether that Nation, or any Nation so conceived and so dedicated, can long endure.

"We are met on a great battlefield of that war. We have come here to dedicate a portion of that field as a final resting place for those who here gave their lives that that Nation might live.

"It is altogether fitting and proper that we should do this.

"But in a larger sense, we can not dedicate, we can not consecrate, we can not hallow this ground. The brave men, living and dead, who struggled here, have consecrated it far above our power to add or detract.

"The world will little note or long remember what we say here; but it can never forget what they did here.

"It is for us, the living, rather to be dedicated here to the unfinished work which they who fought here have, thus far, so nobly advanced.

"It is rather for us to be here dedicated to the great task remaining before us; that from these honored dead we take increased devotion to that cause for which they gave the last full measure of devotion; that we here highly resolve that these dead shall not have died in vain; that this Nation, under God, shall have a new birth of freedom; and that government of the people, by the people and for the people, shall not perish from the earth."

GOLDEN WORDS OF ABRAHAM LINCOLN.

The name that dwells on every tongue
No minstrel needs.

"Gold is good in its place; but living, brave and patriotic men are better than gold."

"God must like the common people, or he would not have made so many of them."

"I am indeed very grateful to the brave men who have been struggling with the enemy in the field."

"This country, with its institutions, belongs to the people who inhabit it."

"Let us have that faith that right makes might, and in that faith let us, to the end, dare to do our duty as we understand it."

"The reasonable man has long since agreed that intemperance is one of the greatest, if not the greatest, of all evils among mankind."

"The purposes of the Almighty are perfect and must prevail, though we erring mortals may fail to accurately perfect them in advance."

"Of the people, when they rise in mass in behalf of the Union and the liberties of their country, truly may it be said: 'The gates of hell can not prevail against them?' "

"I appeal to you again to constantly bear in mind that with you (the people), and not with politicians, not with Presidents, not with officeseekers, but with you, is the question, shall the Union, and shall the liberties of the country be preserved to the last generation."

"General Grant is a copious worker and fighter, but a very meager writer and telegrapher."

"With malice toward none, with charity for all, with firmness in the right as God gives us to see the right, let us strive on to finish the work we are in; to bind up the Nation's wounds; to care for him who shall have borne the battle, and for his widow and orphans; to do all which may achieve and cherish a just and lasting peace among ourselves and with all nations.

GOLDEN ADVICE TO THE AMERICAN YOUTH.

"I owe my success to one single fact, namely: That at the age of twenty-seven I commenced and continued for years the process of daily reading and speaking upon the contents of some historical and scientific book. These off-hand efforts were made sometimes in a corn field, at others in a forest, and, not unfrequently in some distant barn, with the horse and ox for my auditors. It is to this early practice of the great art of oratory that I am indebted for the primary and leading impulses that stimulated me forward, and have shaped and moulded my entire subsequent destiny. Improve, young gentlemen, the superior advantages you here enjoy. Let not a day pass without exercising your powers of speech. There is no power like that of oratory. Caesar controlled men by exciting their fears; Cicero, by captivating their affections and swaying their passions. The influence of one perished with its author, that of the other continues to this day."—Henry Clay.

—Pierpont.

THAT CARTOON OF '91.

[Doubtless there are many persons who will remember the cartoon of Decoration Day for '91, in Puck, in which the artist has pictured " Reconciliation " twining garlands of flowers lovingly around a monument containing the statues of Grant, Sherman and Sheridan, and also one containing those of Lee, Jackson and Johnston, the same garland reaching from North to South, while the woman of the North and the woman of the South, garlanded with wreaths the graves of their dead, casting at the same time suspicious glances towards each other. as the child of the North and the child of the South, in blissful ignorance and loving innocence, exchange flowers from their mother's baskets. The lesson is a beautiful one, and well has the artist portrayed it.]

It was only a simple cartoon—
  But sweet was the lesson it taught,
Of love and tears alike for all,
  Who the battle so bravely fought.
Yes, love and tears, after many years,
  We will strew with the flowers we've brought.

Fling the garlands we twine from North to South;
  Let them float alike o'er all.
So bravely each marched to the cannon's mouth,
  Alike in death to fall.
Whether friend or foe while here below,
  Above there is love for all.

Aye, "a little child the world shall lead."
  We will mingle our flowers in peace;
We will sheathe the sword we no longer need,
  And hatred and anger shall cease.
From the shadow of strife which darkened our life,
  Forever we'll seek release.

Ah! well hath the artist the lesson learned;
  He hath read between the lines;
"Except ye become as a little child,"
  So a garland for all he twines.
While the child of the North with the child of the South,
  The flowers of love combines,

—Lue Semans Hadley.

MEMORIAL DAY.

"Hats off to the veterans on Memorial Day! Carry high the stars and stripes they love so dearly, that God's sunlight may glorify them; that the free winds may be burdened, thanks to them; that the smallest child may see them clearly and add his youthful cheer to the heart-cry that greets them as they pass! Hats off to the battle flags as they are borne silently to the bivouac of the dead!

"Off with your hat as the flag goes by
And let the heart have its say!
You're man enough for a tear in your eye
That you will not wipe away."

"And when the thin blue line has faded in the distance, when the battle flags have been borne out of vision, when the last echo of the bugle has died away, do not, dear boys and girls, when returning to your peaceful homes, forget the duty you owe to the veterans. The honor, the very existence of the nation, depends on their memory being held in loving, grateful remembrance. Every year there are more mounds to decorate. Ere long there will be no old veterans left alone to decorate them. Let the patriotic seeds thus sown continue to bear their harvest with the boys and girls, filling the ranks of the veterans, and continue the beautiful and impressive ceremony of strewing sweet blossoms over the graves of the silent army of the Nation's heroes."

"Give them the chaplets they won in the strife,
Give them the laurels they lost with their life,
Crown in your hearts those dead heroes of ours
And cover them over with beautiful flowers."

—Veteran.

THE BALLOT BOX.

"A weapon that comes down as still
As snowflakes fall upon the sod;
But executes a freeman's will,
As lightning does the will of God;
And from its force nor doors nor locks
Can shield you—'tis the ballot box."

—Anon.

THE BOY FOR ME.

The boy that holds his head erect
And speaks politely—he
Will keep abreast of every good;
Oh, that's the boy for me.
That studies during study time,
And scorns his task to shirk,
Assists his mates—but that same boy
Must play as well as work.

He need not try to be a man,
Nor seek for manly joys.
Oh, no! For what would this world be
Without our gladsome boys?
First at his books, first at his play,
In kite-time fly his kite.
'Tis not a man I'd have him be,
But a roguish boy despite.

The head erect, the speech polite,
  The lesson learned—the play
Enjoyed with youth's delightful zest
  And hope's inspiring ray.
Then, boys, all hold your heads erect,
  And speak politely, too,
While every day your hearts expand
  To become good and true.

Faultless you cannot be, my boy,
  But raise your standard high.
Honor is boyhoods noblest guest—
  Sight her with youth's bright eye.
Do not let your courage fail,
  Though disappointed oft;
Shake out the folds of discontent,
  And keep your eye aloft.

THE MAN WITH THE MUSKET.

Soldiers, pass on from this rage of renown,
  This ant-hill commotion and strife,
Pass by where the marbles and bronzes look down
  With their fast-frozen gestures of life,
On out to the nameless who lie 'neath the gloom
  Of the pitying cypress and pine;
Your man is the man of the sword and the plume,
  But the man of the musket is mine.

I knew him! By all that is noble, I knew
  This commonplace hero I name!
I've camped with him, marched with him, fought with him, too,
  In the swirl of the fierce battle-flame!
Laughed with him, cried with him, taken a part
  Of his canteen and blanket, and know
That the throb of this chivalrous prairie boy's heart
  Was an answering stroke of my own.

I knew him, I tell you! And also I knew,
When he fell on the battle-swept ridge,
That the poor battered body that lay there in blue
  Was only a plank in the bridge,
Over which some should pass to a fame
  That shall shine while the high stars shall shine!
Your hero is known by an echoing name,
  But the man of the musket is mine.

I knew him! All through him the good and the bad
  Ran together and equally free;
But I judge as I trust Christ will judge the brave lad,
  For death made him noble to me!
In the cyclone of war, in the battle's eclipse,
  Life shook out its lingering sands,
And he died with the names that he loved on his lips,
  His musket still grasped in his hands!
Up close to the flag my soldier went down,
  In the salient front of the line.
You may take for your heroes the men of renown,
  But the man of the musket is mine!
                —Rev. Howard S. Taylor, Ill.

NATIVE LAND.

Breathes there the man with soul so dead
Who never to himself hath said,
This is my own, my native land!
Whose heart hath ne'er within him burned,
As home his footsteps he hath turned
From wandering on a foreign strand?
If such there breathe, go, mark him well;
For him no minstrel raptures swell;
High though his titles, proud his name,
Boundless his wealth as wish can claim,
Despite these titles, power, and pelf,
The wretch, concentered all in self,
Living, shall forfeit fair renown,
And, doubly dying, shall go down
To the vile dust from whence he sprung,
Unwept, unhonored and unsung.

—Sir Walter Scott.

THE OLD GUARD.

I heard the ringing bugle-call, the drums that loudly beat,
And country folk were gathered in throngs on every street.
In thoughtful mood, the farmers, with comely country dame,
The joyous lads and lassies, from far and near they came.
While portico and balcony, house-top and window bars
Were decked with loyal mottoes, with waving Stars and Stripes.
I asked a passing soldier—young, fair, erect and strong—
The meaning of the muster, and all that loyal throng.
He gracefully saluted, then proudly did he say,
"The Thirteenth Indiana are off for the war today."

—A. A. McLaughlin, 115 N. Y. Infantry.

WHEN ALL ARE GONE.

"When all are gone, the maimed and weary-hearted,
　　When 'taps' have sounded and the lights are out,
When the last veteran from his friends has parted,
　　And Death has put the valiant force to rout—
Then shall we hear their praise sung aloud;
　　Then will Columbia of her sons be proud."
There sounded the tread of marching feet:
　　Stately, slow, not the haste of retreat;
Colors tossed high in the April breeze
　　And kissed the budding forest trees;
The drum had a voice not heard before,
　　Its throbbing said: "We fight no more!"
We are coming home! Rejoice, Oh land!
　　And thrill to the tread of each valiant band.

—Mrs. N. B. Morange.

And I saw a phantom army come,
With never a sound of fife or drum,
But keeping time to a muffled hum,
    Of wailing and lamentation!
The martyred heroes of Malvern Hill,
Of Gettysburg and Chancellorsville,
The men whose wasted figures fill
    The patriot graves of the Nation.
                      —Bret Harte.

Over a quarter century's passed since when
We organized for war the mounted men,
Departed to the front, to ride and fight,
To battle for the Union they thought right;
Endure all sorts of hardships and yet stay
To see the end or die—it was their way.
From school, from college, farm, shop or trade,
Right cheerfully they joined the Horse-brigade—
Accoutrements and steed each one secured;
Eats his rough rations, smiles as he endured.
Did it to the end, might do it again,
The gallant, armed with rifles, mounted men.
                    —Edward S. Creamer.

The rebels Fort Sumter were storming,
    And treason was flaunting in glee,
Secession's battalions were forming
    To humble the stars of the free;
But up sprang each brave Northern ranger,
    The swords of their fathers they drew;
When freedom's fair land was in danger
    'Twas saved by our Brave Boys in Blue.
                    —M. Victor Staley.

The eagle flew; the flag unfurled!
A shock electric thrilled the world
For oft had liberty been sought,
And oft with blood and suffering bought;
But all who hailed its early day,
Had seen its radiance fade away
In luxury and selfish strife;
But now the Bible gave it life,
And now this truth shone like the sun
That liberty and God are one.
                    —I. W. Dunbar.

Thy sacred leaves. fair Freedom's flower,
Shall ever float on dome and tower,
To all their heavenly colors true.
The blackening frost or crimson dew,
And God love us as we love thee,
Thrice holy Flower of Liberty,
Then hail the banner of the free
The Starry Flower of Liberty.
                    —Oliver Wendell Holmes.

INSPIRING QUOTATIONS AND EXTRACTS FROM PATRIOTIC ADDRESSES.

To prepare for war is one of the most effectual means of preserving peace.

Interwoven is the love of liberty with every ligament of the heart.

Without virtue and without regularity, the finest talents and the most brilliant accomplishments can never gain the respect and conciliate the esteem of the truly valuable part of mankind.—George Washington.

"Washington had conquered. It was the victory of a great and good man in a great and good cause."

Humanity has won its suit in America, so that liberty will never more be without an asylum.—Marquis de Lafayette.

In my opinion there never was a good war or a bad peace.

Energy and persistence conquer all things.—Benjamin Franklin.

Of those men who have overturned the liberties of republics, the greatest number have begun their career by paying an obsequious court to the people; commencing demagogues and ending tyrants.—Alexander Hamilton.

Sir, I would rather be right than to be President.—Henry Clay.

Every man must be for the United States or against it. There can be no neutrals in this war—only patriots or traitors.—Stephen A. Douglass, 1861.

Force is all conquering, but its victories are short-lived.

Knavery and flattery are blood relations.—Abraham Lincoln.

One flag, one land, one heart, one hand,
One nation ever more!—Oliver Wendell Holmes.

"Show me the generals and statesmen who stood foremost, that I may bend to them in reverence."

Intellect is stronger than cannon.—Theodore Parker.

Yesterday the greatest question was decided that was ever debated in America. A resolution was passed without one dissenting colony, that these United Colonies are, and of right ought to be, free and independent States.—John Adams.

"The Gordian knot is cut," exclaimed John Adams, in 1776, when he was informed that Congress recommended all the colonies to form independent governments.

I rejoice in nothing more than this movement, recently so prominently developed, of placing a starry banner above every school house. I have been charged with too sentimental appreciation of the flag. I will not enter upon any defense. God pity the American citizen who does not love it, who does not see in it the story of our great free institutions, and the hope of the home as well as the Nation.—Benjamin Harrison.

We hold these truths to be self-evident; that all men are created equal; that they are endowed by their Creator with certain inalienable rights; that among these are life, liberty and the pursuit of happiness.—Thomas Jefferson.

A star for every State, and a State for every star.—Robert C. Winthrop.

If we are true to our country, in our day and generation, and those who come after us shall be true to it also, assuredly shall we elevate her to a pitch of prosperity and happiness, of honor and power, never yet reached by any nation beneath the sun.—Col. Geo. T. Balch.

I will face the enemy until I die.—Gen. Nicholas Herkimer.

What the Puritans gave the world was not thought, but action. One on God's side is a majority.—Wendell Phillips.

> The union of hearts, the union of hands,
> And the flag of our Union forever.—G. P. Morris.

Let the rising generation be inspired with an ardent love for their country, an unquenchable thirst for liberty, and a profound reverence for the Constitution and the Union. Let the American youth never forget that they possess a noble inheritance, bought by the toils and sufferings and blood of their ancestors—Story.

> Go ring the bells, and fire the guns,
> And fling the starry banner out;
> Shout "Freedom!" till your lisping ones
> Give back their cradle shout.—Whittier.

I will be as harsh as truth and as uncompromising as justice.—William Lloyd Garrison.

Before men made us citizens, great Nature made us men.
Slow are the steps of Freedom, but her feet turn never backward.—Lowell.

> "Let independence be our boast
> Ever mindful what it cost."

The Declaration of Independence, with a voice of an angel from heaven. "put to his mouth the sounding alchemy," and proclaimed universal emancipation upon earth.—John Quincy Adams.

> "Under spread ensigns moving high
> In slow but firm battalions."

Patriotism is not the mere holding of our flag unfurled, but making it the goodliest, grandest, and greatest in the world.—W. F.

We join ourselves to no party that does not carry the flag and keep step to the music of the Union.—Rufus Choate.

> "Men who their duties know,
> But know their rights, and knowing, dare maintain."

> America! half brother of the world!
> With something good and bad of every land,
> Greater than thee have lost their seat—
> Greater scarce none can stand.—P. J. Bailey.

He that does good for good's sake, seeks neither praise nor reward, though sure of both at last.—William Penn.

Every freeman was a host and felt as though himself were he on whose sole arm hung victory.

Love is never lost. If not reciprocated it will flow back and soften and purify the heart.—Washington Irving.

Character is higher than intellect; a great soul will be strong to live, as well as strong to think.—Ralph Waldo Emerson.

Then conquer we must, for our cause it is just,
And this be our motto, "In God is our trust."

I love America and every thing American.—Mrs. Levi P. Morton.

We judge ourselves by what we feel capable of doing, while others judge us by what we have already done.—Henry W. Longfellow.

There is room in this country for only one flag, and "Old Glory" must head the procession, or it can not march.—Chauncey M. Depew.

The phrase, "public office is a public trust," has of late become common property.—Charles Sumner.

Every good citizen makes his country's honor his own, and cherishes it, not only as precious, but as sacred. He is willing to risk his life in its defense, and is conscious that he gains protection while he gives it. Our Federal Union, it must be preserved.—Andrew Jackson.

Oh! never shall the land forget
How gushed the life-blood of her brave,—
Gushed warm with hope and courage yet
Upon the soil they sought to save.—Bryant.

Then said the mother to the son,
And pointed to his shield—
"Come with it when the battle's done,
Or on it from the field."—Robert Montgomery.

I am not a Virginian, but an American.

I repeat it, sir; we must fight! An appeal to arms and to the God of Hosts is all that is left us.

Our chains are forged. Their clanking may be heard on the plains of Boston.

Is life so dear, or peace so sweet, as to be purchased at the price of chains and slavery? Forbid it Almighty God! I know not what course others may take; but as for me, give me liberty or give me death!—Patrick Henry.

There are two freedoms, the false, where a man is free to do what he likes; the true, where a man is free to do what he ought.—Charles Kingsley.

Peace hath her victories,
No less renowned than war.—Milton.

The proper qualities of a general are judgment and deliberation.—Gen. Benj. Lincoln.

The kindred blood which flows in the veins of American citizens, the mingled blood which they have shed in defense of their sacred rights, consecrate their union.—James Madison.

What I am, I owe to my country.

The true prosperity and greatness of a Nation is to be found in the elevation and education of its laborers.

I do not believe in luck in war any more than luck in business. Luck is a small matter; may affect a battle or a movement, but not a campaign or a career.

We believe that we have a good government worthy fighting for, and, if need be, dying for.—U. S. Grant.

School houses are the Republic's line of fortifications.

Next in importance to freedom and justice is popular education, without which neither justice nor freedom can be permanently maintained.

There are some things I am afraid of: I am afraid to do a mean thing.

The children of today will be the architects of our country's destiny in 1900.—James A. Garfield.

When Washington declined a military escort on the occasion of his inauguration (1789), he said, "I require no guard but the affection of the people."—Edward Everett.

Under God we are determined that wheresoever, whensoever, or howsoever we shall be called to make our exit, we will die free men.—Josiah Quincy.

> "The soldier's warfare all is done,
> Life's wandering marches o'er;
> God gave him rest among the blest
> In heaven for evermore."

The British summoned the garrison to surrender, or no quarter would be given. Colonel Greene replied, "We ask no quarter, nor will we give any."

> Such is the patriots boast, where'er we roam,
> His first, best country ever is home.—Goldsmith.

Necessity is the argument of tyrants; it is the creed of slavery.—William Pitt.

Be just, and fear not; let the ends thou aim'st at, be thy country's, thy God's, and truth's.

I love my country's good, with a respect more tender, more holy and profound, than my whole life.—Shakespeare.

> Then join hands, brave Americans all;
> By uniting we stand, dividing we fall.—John Dickinson.

It's faith in something, an enthusiasm for something that makes a life worth looking at.—Holmes.

I love freedom better than slavery. I will speak her words; I will listen to her music; I will acknowledge her impulses; I will stand beneath her flag; I will fight in her ranks; and when I do so, I shall find myself surrounded by the great, the wise, the good, the brave, the noble, of every land.—E. D. Baker.

Not the stars and stripes, but what they stand for needs enphasizing.—E. L. Hendricks.

But the colonial time-piece kept ticking, ticking, to the pressure of the English Government, the giant wheels playing calmly, till 1775, when there was a strange stir and buzz within the case. But the sixtieth minute came and the clock struck. The world heard: The battle of Lexington, one; the Declaration of Independence, two; the surrender of Burgoyne, three; the siege of Yorktown, four; the treaty of Paris, five; the inauguration of Washington, six; and then it was sunrise of the new day, of which we have seen yet only the glorious forenoon.—Thomas Starr King.

"An age like this demands
Great minds, brave hearts,
And strong and willing hands;
Men whom the lust of office can not kill;
Men whom the spoils of office can not buy;
Men who possess opinions and a will;
Men who can legislate and dare not lie."

Even the celestial hemisphere has caught the inspiration by an occasional patriotic display of the Aurora Borealis illuminating the northern horizon with an immense outline of the stars and stripes in blue, red and white light, studded with dazzling white crystal stars in a wavy sea of etherial blue, suspended from the heavens by golden halyards, held, as it were, by unseen hands of our departed heroes, who died that patriotism and the dear old flag might live in the hearts of their countrymen.—W. F.

The mountain nymph, sweet Liberty.—John Milton.

Oh, God of our fathers! this banner must shine
Where battle is hottest, in warfare divine;
The cannon has thundered, the bugle has blown,
We fear not the summons, we fight not alone.
Oh, lead us till wide from the gulf to the sea
The land shall be sacred to freedom and Thee.
With love for the oppressed, with blessings for scars,
One country, one banner—the stripes and the stars.
—[Edna Dean Proctor..

These are the times that try men's souls.—Thomas Paine.

Lay me down and save the flag.—Col. James Mulligan.

With patriotism in our hearts and with the flag of our country in the hands of our children there is no danger of anarchy and there will be no danger to the Union.—Wm. McKinley, Jr.

Let us give thanks for sentiment—that sentiment that makes us love and reverence our emblem as represented in our own flag. No child in the public schools at New Orleans can enter the school house without passing under the flag and this is due to the influence of women in a rebel city.

The price of our flag is broken hearts and blood and the flag belongs to women, since they gave their only begotten sons to save the country. —Mrs. E. Florence Barker, First National President W. R. C.

I have served my country under the flag of the Union for more than fifty years; and as long as God permits me to live I will defend that flag with my sword, even if my own State assails it.—Lieut.-Gen. Winfield Scott.

> Patriots in peace assert the people's right,
> With noble stubbornness resisting might.—Dryden.

> Years have left no scar of battle,
> But at times I seem to see
> Those bold heroes on King's Mountain
> Turn a nation's destiny.—S. B. K.

If I had my way I would hang the flag in every school room and attempt to impress upon all the supreme value of their inheritance.—Prof. Andrew S. Draper.

A nation without a national government is an awful spectacle.

I am unmoved by any rancor or spirit of hatred, God forbid; but I am a Union soldier, and I love my flag, and I say here, and I will say everywhere, that for Americans there is but one flag—the flag of Bunker Hill, and Saratoga, and Yorktown; the flag of Lundy's Lane, Lake Champlain, and Erie, and New Orleans; the flag of Scott, McDonough, Perry and Jackson; the flag of Lincoln, the flag of Hancock, the flag of Grant, the flag of Washington. It is the only flag which represents the right, and in our charity let us not forget the difference between right and wrong.—Gen. Daniel E. Sickles.

But the men and women who were the actors during the great Civil War did not do your work. That lies before you. You are living in a grand time; rise to the full measure of your possibilities and your life will be sublime. A true Christian character is the sure foundation of a successful life. Store your mind with useful knowledge. Set the glorious flag flying everywhere; lift it over every school-house. Teach your children what it symbolizes, what the principles at the foundation of our government are. Eschew evil, fear God, and this Republic will continue to be what it now is, the fairest among the nations of the earth.—Annie Witenmyer.

Who could not love and respect our beautiful flag of America, and say, long may it wave over the land of the free and the true? The bravery we boast let it not be the love of war and bloodshed of our fellowmen, because they do not entertain the same opinion and all have one mind and spirit as we have. But to this end, gentle law-makers, God-fearing men, can keep the peace and win many on the side of truth and virtue. The United States, the States that are united, must stand together as one —"United we stand, divided we fall." The good and the true must hold it together. Union must be the watchword. Love of country is not love of party.—Mrs. J. M. D. F.

> Oh, sons of Massachusetts, first to rally, first to die!
> The patriot fire within your hearts, its light within your eye,
> First gave to freedom's faltering heart the promise of the cheer.
> —Anna Phillips Clarke.

"England may as well dam up the waters of the Nile with bullrushes as to fetter the step of Freedom, more proud and firm in this youthful land than where she treads the sequestered glens of Scotland or couches herself among the magnificent mountains of Switzerland."—Lydia Maria Child.

> "Spurn, spurn despair! be great, be free!
> With giant strength arise;
> Stretch, stretch thy pinions, Liberty,
> Thy flag plant in the skies."

>   And everywhere
>   The slender, graceful spars
>   Pose aloft in the air,
>   And at the masthead,
>   White, blue, red,
>   A flag unrolls—the Stripes and Stars.
>   Oh! when the wanderer, lonely, friendless,
>   In foreign harbors shall behold
>   The flag unrolled,
>   'Twill be as a friendly hand
>   Stretched out from his native land,
>   Filling his heart with memories sweet and endless!
>   —Henry Wadsworth Longfellow.

There are two things holy—the flag, which represents military honor, and the law, which represents the national right.—Victor Hugo.

>   "Our Union is river, lake, ocean, and sky,
>   Man breaks not the medal, when God cuts the die;
>   Though darkened with sulphur, tho' cloven with steel,
>   The blue arch will brighten, the waters will heal."

Let our object be our country, our whole country, and nothing but our country; and, by the blessing of God, may that country itself become a vast and splendid monument, not of oppression and terror, but of wisdom, of peace, and of liberty, upon which the world may gaze with admiration forever.

On the diffusion of education among the people, rests the preservation and perepetuation of our free institutions.

Whatever makes men good Christians, makes them good citizens.

I was born an American; I live an American; I shall die an American. One country, one constitution, one destiny.—Daniel Webster.

There is great need of educated men in our public life, but it is the need of educated men with patriotism.—Grover Cleveland.

The real and true patriot is not the man that seeks after vainglory, but he who tries to make his country better by his conduct, and his way of living, and is proud of his country and people, and does what is needful to uphold and maintain the laws.—Rev. E. C. Balles.

Democracy means not, "I am as good as you are," but "You are as good as I am."—Theo. Parker.

John Adams was the orator of that Revolution, the Revolution in which a nation was born.—Choate.

>   Take from your flag its folds of gloom,
>   And let it float undimmed above,
>   Till over all our vales shall bloom,
>   The sacred colors that we love.—Phoebe Carey.

>   "Between the patriot and the politician
>   There is this difference known:
>   The former seeks his country's good
>   The latter seeks his own."

"Men who are animated with heroic sentiments, and imbued with patriotic spirit, invariably live longer than others. The fifty-six signers of the Declaration of Independence arrived at a great age, and all died more calmly, than the same number of men ever engaged in any important national event."

I'm tired of being told it is a crime to use the word American. If it is a crime for me to say that I owe my first allegiance to this country, then I am certainly a criminal. America is for Americans, no matter whether they be naturalized or native born.—Kate Field.

> "The victory, like a midnight sun,
> Burst forth with dazzling glory,
> But after the fierce triumph won
> We knew a darker story."

"Our flag is the banner of dawn. It means Liberty; the galley slave, the poor oppressed conscript, the down-trodden creature of foreign despotism, sees in the American flag that very promise and prediction of God, "The people which sat in darkness saw a great light, and to them which sat in the region and shadow of death light is sprung up."

What can any man do against our flag? Let him have mounted ever so high upon the roll of honor, let him have entrenched himself ever so strongly in the affection of the people; if he lifts his hand against the flag he falls at once.—Gen. Harrison at Old Forge, N. Y., July 26, 1896.

Our flag carries American ideas, American history and American feelings. Beginning with the colonies, and coming down to our time, in its sacred heraldry, in its glorious insignia, it has gathered and stored chiefly this supreme idea: Divine right of liberty in man. Every color means liberty; every form of star and beam or stripe of light means liberty; not lawlessness, not license, but organized institutional liberty—liberty through law, and laws for liberty. It is a whole national history. It is the Constitution. It is the government. It is the free people that stand in the government on the constitution.—Rev. Henry Ward Beecher.

> So through the night rode Paul Revere,
> And so through the night went his cry of alarm
> To every Middlesex village and farm.—Longfellow.

What eloquence do the stars breathe when their full significance is known; a new constellation, union, perpetuity, a covenant against oppression, justice, equality, subordination, courage and purity.—Rear Admiral George H. Preble.

Death never comes too soon, if necessary in defense of the liberties of our country.—Judge Story.

I will treasure up the memory of the Nation's dead and on every suitable occasion, as long as life lasts, will present them anew to the youth of this country, as noble examples of heroism and patriotism.—General William T. Sherman.

"In all the trade of war, no feat
Is nobler than a brave retreat."

It is a matter of great anxiety and concern to me that the slave trade is sometimes perpetrated under the flag of liberty, our dear noble Stars and Stripes, to which virtue and glory have been constant standard-bearers.—LaFayette.

"Men of action, men of might,
Stern defenders of the right."

How I do wish that you could have looked down upon us when we threw the "Stars and Stripes" to the breeze at 12 o'clock on the 26th. Our chaplain thanked God for having brought us from our place of danger, and prayed for our country, that our flag might long continue to wave over a united and happy people. The flag was then raised, the command presenting arms, and the band playing "The Star Spangled Banner," after which three cheers were given for the flag and three for the Union. [Extract from a letter to a friend.]—Robert Anderson, Ft. Sumter, S. C., December 30, 1860.

"And now the work of life and death
Hung on the passing of a breath;
The fire of conflict burned within:
The battle trembled to begin."
So long ago, a mother's eyes
 Weep now but scanty tears,
Fell one, who, under Southern skies,
 Has slumbered deep for years.
He had his loss and his reward,
 Both in a sure release;
His loss, the victor's shining sword;
 His guerdon, endless peace.
—N. B. M.

Braver men never smiled at danger than those who fought under the Stars and Stripes, and whenever Death spread his banquet, "New Hampshire" furnished many guests. God bless forever! the living and the dead, who under the flag of our country marched to glory or the grave. —Governor Harriman.

Thank God! the struggle's over, peace reigns in all our land.
United now as brothers, forever let us stand;
One flag, one country—Union—no North, South, East or West,
Each vying with each other to do the very best;
With millions of defenders to rally at its call,
"Old Glory" is an emblem that truthful speaks to all;
We love to look upon it as it proudly floats on high,
No star is darkly blotted, no stripe but of royal dye.
—B. Read Wales.

"Goodness and greatness are not means but ends.
Hath he not always treasures, always friends,
 The good great man?"

A thousand and ten thousand times, no! "Put up thy sword," said the Divine Master, "they that conquer by the sword shall perish by the sword."

What, then, will you do, men who saved the Republic? The remedy is in your hands. Place the flag over every school building and in every school room in the land. Then teach your children and the children of all nations flocking to your standard, those immortal principles of free government of which the Stars and Stripes is but the sign and symbol.—Kate Brownlee Sherwood.

"The sounds of war are silent now,
  We call no man our foe;
But soldier hearts cannot forget
  The scenes of long ago.
Dear are the ones who stood with us
  To struggle or to die;
No one can oftener breathe their names
  Or love them more than I."

Mother of States and unpolluted men,
Virginia fitly named from England's manly queen.
—Lowell.

A quarter of a century has passed since the Great Commander of the Union Army received the surrender of Lee at Appomattox, and as he stretched his hand out to take the hand of Lee, he said to him and to a weary Nation tired of war: "Let us have peace." And we wish peace from one end of the land to the other; and we wish at the same time to see the flag we love revered wherever it floats.—R. A. Alger.

Over Barbara Freitchie's grave
Flag of Freedom and Union wave!
Peace and order and beauty draw
Round thy symbol of light and law;
And ever the stars above look down
On thy stars below in Fredericktown.
—John G. Whittier.

"Every act of noble sacrifice for the country, every instance of patriotic devotion to her cause, has its beneficial influence."

The past is past; the wild flowers bloom where charging squadrons met;
And though we keep war's memories green, why not the cause forget,
And have, while battle-stains fade out 'neath heaven's pitying tears,
One Land, One Flag, one brotherhood, through all the coming years?
—Thomas S. Collier.

"There's a midnight darkness changing into grey;
Men of thought, and men of action, clear the way!"

Patriotic men cannot be produced in homes where patriotic women do not exist. So, if one limits the consideration of women's patriotism to the influence which it should exert in her home, a standing committee on patriotism ought to commend itself to the approval of the entire Nation.—May Wright Sewall.

If in love for our country you share
  And "The Star Spangled Banner" are versed in,
You will know when the "bombs burst in air,"
  'Twas a national air they burst in.

—Judge.

"On the sword, therefore, we are compelled to rely for protection."

We want it distinctly understood that there is but one nation here, and that is the American nation.—Rev. Father Dalton.

What is my arm, or my life, compared with the safety of my country. —Sentiments of a Dying Soldier.

"Sadly, dumbly asking quarter,
For the furious fight is done,
And the patriots stand as victors
In the last light of the sun."

Make the best use of the public schools by making systematic instructions in patriotic citizenship the chief part of the course of study. —Thomas Hunter, President New York Normal College.

"Now for the fight!
Now for the cannon-peal!
Forward! through blood and toil, and cloud and fire!"

Education is the bulwark of our national liberties.
The public school is the nursery of patriotism. Its best fruits are true Americans, and its crowning glory the making of loyal and intelligent citizens.—Rev. A. N. Whitmarsh.

Our "White Squadron" is something more than a harmless symbol of national power and pride. It is not a flock of doves. It means peace only when that is consistent with justice and honor. Harsh precautions, but, unhappily, necessary for the well-being of the Republic.—Uncle Sam's Church.

"God bless New Hampshire, from her granite peaks
Once more the voice of Stack and Langdon speaks."

While offering peace, sincere and just,
In Heaven we place a manly trust,
That truth and justice will prevail,
And every scheme of bondage fail.
—F. Hopkinson.

The American patriot has a different object in life from the Athenian patriot, or almost any other kind of patriot who ever lived before our government was founded. These other patriots defended themselves and their own children; they fought to hold their own power and the privileges of their own class. The American patriot lives for the great commonwealth. He does not defend merely his own rights; he does not vote for his own rights or his own interest. Show him what is best for all the people. He stands to defend and serve them. So Washington and the founders of the Republic seemed to command. So Abraham Lincoln and the men who died in the Civil War, urge. What American youth will not heed this heroic call?—Chas. F. Dole.

"Full many a heart is aching with mingled joy and pain,
For those who went so proudly forth, and may not come again."

To have been soldiers in the cause of our country and fought its battles, won its victories and perpetuated its renown, and to be recognized as such, is the grandest insignia of life.—Geo. B. Loud.

Teach the youth in the kindergarten to respect and honor the flag of their country; it will be the stepping-stone to loyal Christian citizenship. Instruct them to reverently salute the flag of the Union and the lesson it teaches. The effect of the salute will be magical in developing and quickening their desire for more knowledge in the history of our country, and fill their souls with a lofty patriotism that will remain indelible in their hearts, when they reach manhood and womanhood.—Mrs. Eliza A. Blaker, Supt. Indianapolis Kindergarten and Domestic and Normal Training Schools.

> "So out of shop and farm-house,
> From shore and inland glen,
> Thick as the bees in clover-time,
> Are swarming armed men."

I note with a feeling of personal pride the teaching of patriotism in the public schools of our own dear land. The W. R. C. has proclaimed the key-note of its power in the development of patriotic teaching and stands to-day without a peer among the organizations of woman in the grand and glorious work for our beloved country.—Mrs. Jennie Myerhoof.

> Little knew they all the valor
> That assaulting band would show;
> Men who fight for home and honor
> Strike with God to guide the blow.
> —S. B. K.

The bravest and best men with whom I came in contact during two great conflicts were Christian men, and I believe the better Christian a man is, the braver, truer and nobler he is in private and public life. I do not see how a man can be brave or useful unless he is a Christian. —General James Longstreet.

Love your country, reverence its laws, take pride in perpetuating the name and fame of its defenders, be good citizens, and in this promote the glory and prosperity of our own beloved America.—Mrs. Millie B. Loud.

We are Americans; we believe in American principles; and Americans should know and love their country, because in America there is more genuine liberty and happiness than in any other country under the sun —John S. Koontz.

> "To arms! replied the plains,
> The hot blood throbbing through their veins,
> For millions rallied with the vow,
> We strike for freedom surely now."

I am going into Mobile Bay in the morning if "God is my leader," as I hope he is.—Extract from a letter written home by Armiral D. G. Farragut, just before the battle of Mobile.

> "Long and bloody was the fray
> Ere Columbia gained the day;
> Lowly many a hero lay
> Dying to be free."

Should anything befall me you must console yourself by knowing that I laid down my life for my country. For, upon entering its service, when a boy, I dedicated my life to that country.—Extract from a letter written home by Rear Admiral George Brown, Commander of U. S. Gunboat "Itasca," off Mobile, August 4, 1864.

The laws of war award to spies the punishment of death. It would therefore be difficult to assign a reason why Major Andre should have been exempted from that fate.

[Execution of Andre, Saturday, October 2, 1780.]

All I request of you, gentlemen, is that, while I acknowledge the propriety of my sentence, you will bear me witness that I die like a brave man.—Andre's Last Word.s

> Columbia, my country, thy stars are unfurled,
> Mild beaming with peace o'er a jarring world;
> And well may we joy that Atlantic's broad ocean
> Doth roll between thee and old Europe's commotion.
> Thy broad-spreading empire, oh, long may it be
> The home of the patriot, the land of the free!
> —M. S. S.

Treachery, though at first very cautious, in the end betrays itself.—Livy.

> To-day beneath our Nation's flag,
> The old red, white and blue,
> A band of noble women work
> In a cause both just and true:
> To aid and succor those who fought
> To save our honored land,
> For home and freedom, God and right,
> Those earnest women stand.
> —Geo. C. Davis.

Our Country. In her intercourse with foreign nations, may she always be in the right, but our Country right or wrong.—Decatur.

The first lesson of patriotism should be taught at the mother's knee where the innocent lips are taught to lisp "Our Father, who art in Heaven." Teach the children to love the word "country." Teach them that the noblest act of a noble life is to die, if need be, in its defense. Then insist that the lessons at the school be befitting the children of American citizens.—Mrs. Julia S. Conklin, Ind.

> "Then staggered by the shot, we saw their serried columns reel,
> And fall as falls the bearded grain beneath the reaper's steel."

> "Those heroes
> Around whose memory clings
> The glory of King's Mountain,
> Cowpens and Eutaw Springs."

The noble Nation is before my soul's vision. Giant in stature, comely in feature, buoyant in the freshness of morning youth, matronly in prudent stepping, the ethereal breezes of liberty waving with loving touch her tresses, she is, no one seeing her doubts, the queen, the conqueror, the mistress, the teacher of coming ages.

To her keeping the Creator has entrusted a great continent, whose shores two oceans lave, rich in nature's gifts, inclosing useful and precious minerals, fertile in soil, salubrious in air, beauteous in vesture. For long centuries He held in reserve this region of His predilection, awaiting a propitious moment in humanity's evolutions to bestow it upon man, when man was ready to receive it. Her children have come from all countries, bearing with them the ripest fruit of thought, labor and experience. Adding thereto high aspirations and generous impulses, they have built up a new world of humanity. This world embraces the hopes, the ambitions, the dreamings of humanity's priests and seers. To its daring in the face of progress, to its sufferings at the shrine of liberty, there seems to be no limit; and yet, prosperity, order, peace, spread over its vast area their sheltered wings.

The Nation of the future! Need I name it? Your hearts quiver loving it—

> "My country, 'tis of thee,
> Sweet land of liberty,
> Of thee I sing."
> —Archbishop Ireland at Opening of Columbian Exposition.

Yes, his sun has set forever. Loyalty's gentle voice can no longer wake thrills of joy along the tuneless chords of his mouldering heart. Yet patriots and lovers of liberty who still linger on the shores of time rise and bless his memory; and millions yet unborn will in after times rise to deplore his death, and cherish as a household word his deathless name.—General John A. Logan, on the death of Abraham Lincoln.

> "For a voice struck through the sunlight,
> Through the deafening roar of war,
> With its call of on and upward!
> Though no man the speaker saw."

When Old Glory kisses the vagrant winds, the fingers of one hand would doubtless number those who knew the origin of the American flag. The children of the present generation will be wiser, however, and when their children come upon the scene of action, there will scarcely be a home sheltered by the starry emblem with inmates so ignorant that they will not know its history.—Isabel Worrell Ball.

> "Where 'mid the columns war's red eagles fly,
> We swear to do or die."

What the country needs to-day is good citizens, whether they be voters or not. Citizens who are familiar with these great bulwarks of American liberty—the Declaration of Independence and the Constitution of the United States. Every woman should have a copy of the Constitution and study it. How can we support that of which we have no knowledge? —Ellen S. Mussey, Washington, D. C.

> State's rights must be respected;
> The Union must be preserved.
> —Charles Carroll.

Freedom is recreated year by year,
In hearts wide open on the Godward side,
In soul's calm cadence as the whirling sphere,
In minds that sway the future like a tide.
No broadest creeds can hold her, and no codes;
She chooses men for her august abodes,
Building them fair and fronting to the dawn.

Our country hath a gospel of her own
To preach and practice before the world—
The freedom and divinity of man,
The glorious claims of human brotherhood—
Which to pay nobly, as a freeman should,
Gains the soul wealth that will not fly away—
And the soul's fealty to none but God.
—Lowell.

They left of all my tribe
Nor man, nor child, nor thing of living birth;
No! not the dog that watched my household hearth
Escaped that night of blood upon these plains.
—Campbell.

No traitor at midnight shall pierce in rest,
No alien at noonday shall stab us abreast.
—Proctor.

With no guide but God, and no constitution but the Bible, our forefathers worked out upon this continent, after many hardships and trials and tribulations, the problem of the equality of all men before the law. They founded instiutions which have withstood the test of foreign invasions, of political passions, of party strifes, of individual ambition, and the shock of the mightiest civil war the world has ever seen. The influence of their successful experiment, following the line of fraternal blood back to the countries from which they came, have revolutionized and liberalized the governments of the globe. The triumph of the principles of civil and religious liberty upon this continent, the beneficial effects of the common school, and the one universal diffusion of education have done more than all other agencies in uplifting mankind to higher places of independence and happiness.—Hon. Chauncey Depew.

The sun of liberty is set; you must light up the candles of industry and economy.—Franklin.

"The maid who binds her warrior's sash
  With smile that well her pain dissembles,
The while beneath the drooping lash
  One starry teardrop hangs and trembles,
    Though heaven alone records the tear,
    And fame shall never know her story—
Her heart has shed a drop as dear
  As e'er bedewed the field of glory.

The wife who girds her husband's sword
  'Mid little ones who weep or wonder,
And bravely speaks the cheering word,
  What though her heart be rent asunder,
Doomed nightly in her dreams to hear
  The bolts of death around him rattle,
Hath shed as sacred blood as e'er
  Was poured upon the field of battle."

"Hamilton, though carried off in the prime of life, had lived long enough for glory."

"All nature sings wildly the song of the free,
The red, white and blue float o'er land and o'er sea;
The white—in each billow that breaks on the shore,
The blue in the arching that canopies o'er
The land of our birth, in its glory outspread—
And sunset dies deepen and glow into red;
Day fades into night and the red stripe retires,
But stars o'er the blue light their sentinel fires;
And though night be gloomy, with clouds overspread,
Each star holds its place in the field overhead;
When scatter the clouds and the tempest is through,
We count every star in the field of the blue."

To be prepared for war is one of the most effectual means of preserving peace.—Washington.

Beware of the man who puts his conduct above his conscience, his party above his country. I don't mean or care to argue that it is necessary that a man shall sacrifice any private duty to be true to his country, or prevent any citizen of the United States to be true to his conscience. Let every man entertain his conviction and leave his neighbor alone. —Henry Watterson.

We live in the consequences of past action.—Hodge.

> Lord of the universe!
>   Shield us and guide us,
> Trusting Thee always,
>   Through shadow and sun,
> Thou hast united us,
>   Who shall divide us?
> Keep us, Oh, keep us,
>   The "many in one."
> Up with our banner bright,
>   Sprinkled with starry light,
> Spread its fair emblem
>   From mountain to shore,
> While through the sounding sky
> Loud rings the Nation's cry,
> Union and liberty!
>   One evermore.
>   —O. W. Holmes.

What can alone ennoble fight?
A noble cause.
                              —Campbell.

"We believe that unborn generations of Americans will be imbued, in the hour of national peril, with the same generous, patriotic impulse which inspired the patriots of the two great historic periods of our country; the one creating national independence in 1776, and the other preserving it through the storms of fratricidal war."

The American flag has never been trailed in the dust by foreign or domestic foe. Wherever it has floated to the breeze, in every sea and upon every land, it has been welcomed by all people, of all nations, as the inspiration to humanity, to society, to the attainment of equal rights. Let the old flag speak to the children in the schools from one end of the land to the other. Let this symbol utter the voice of freedom upon every festive occasion.—Sarah C. Mink.

> "Along the dusty roads in haste
>   The eager columns come,
> With flash of sword and musket's gleam,
>   The bugle and the drum."

"Men of thought! be up and stirring, night and day;
Sow the seed—withdraw the curtain—clear the way!"

> Granite and marble and granite,
>   Corridor, column and dome;
> A Capitol huge as a planet,
>   And mighty as marble-built Rome.
>   —Capitol, U. S.

By representing the characters of great men and women in the making of American history, young people learn to realize that they are a part of the union, and there comes to them a sense of responsibility for its future, and a desire to share in its political life. If we would grow patriotism, we must sow the seeds of patriotism, and the most fruitful seeds are the words and deeds of our patriotic forefathers.—Bishop Samuel Fellows.

>Fraternity, union, now and forever,
>Between us again shall discord come never.
>The old flag above us is wondrously beautiful,
> Brighter and lovelier it seems every day,
>More glorious than ever, for under it, dutiful,
> Stand to defend it, both the blue and the gray.
>   —Blue and the Gray.

"History is the cyclic poem written by Time upon the memories of men."

>"Right and Native Land," their watch word—
>Swift they sped, at country's call,
>Pulled th' sword from out its scabbard,
>Ere they'd see their flagstaff fall.
>   —Eliza Hammond Odneal.

Patriotic instruction should begin in the home. Under the formative care of the best of teachers, a good mother, the elements that go to build up a patriotic spirit will be instilled. She will teach her children the national hymns and patriotic songs, she will tell them the story of that sturdy band of Puritans, who planted the seeds of American civilization, and upon Plymouth's sacred rock laid the corner-stone of the Nation. She will tell them of the supreme patriot, he who was "first in war, first in peace, and first in the hearts of his countrymen," and of that distinguished line of patriots down to our day. She will teach them how grand a thing it is to acquire the principles of obedience to law, of love and veneration for the stars and stripes as the emblem of liberty and national supremacy. Every child should be taught the origin of the flag, when it was adopted, what trials it has encountered, and what blessings preserved. It should be in every home to be cherished, loved and honored. Let the Nation be a nursery of men and principles such as inspired the founders of the government.—Mrs. Louise Barnum Robbins, Mich.

The soldier who resented your insult to the Stars and Stripes was born under its folds, and his father before him. He still retains a respect and affection for it, and an officer of the Confederate Army who has no higher appreciation of the sentiment of our people than you appear to have, by trailing the Stars and Stripes in the dust, is not fit to be on my staff."—Stonewall Jackson.
(Reprimand to an officer.)

>"Thus spake the patriot in his latest sigh,
>'My duty done, I do not fear to die.'"

Its stripes of red, eternal dyed with heart streams of all lands;
Its white, the snow-capped hills, that hide in storm their upraised hands;
Its blue, the ocean waves that beat round freedom's circled shore;
Its stars, the print of angels' feet that burn forevermore.
                                  —James Whitcomb Riley.

> Here sleep the brave, who sink to rest
> By all their country's wishes blest.
> —Collins.

> If we only strive to be pure and true,
> To each of us all there will come an hour
> When the tree of life shall burst into flower,
> And rain at our feet a glorious dower
> Of something grander than ever we knew.
> —Burnside.

Yes, our flag was newly woven, every stripe and every star,
With the cannon balls for shuttles, in the roaring loom of war;
When our gallant weavers dyed it, with their manhood in each hue,
White for honor, red for courage, and for faithfulness the blue.
—[Howard S. Taylor.

Sink or swim, live or die, survive or perish, I give my hand and heart to this vote.—Peyton Randolph.

It is needless to remind you that national greatness depends upon intelligent God-loving patriotism that must spring from love of native land, and obedience to her laws. A true patriot is a devout patriot, and America's eminence to-day among the nations of the earth is due to her devotion to the same stirring battle-cry, "for God and native land." Our country's flag is the symbol of liberty! the aegis for the oppressed, the foe to ignorance and superstition, and the harbinger of civil and religious liberty.—Mrs. W. F. Kuhn, Mo.

> "Words pass as wind, but where great deeds are done,
> A power abides, transfused from sire to son."

As the days roll by and year succeeds year, the memories of the Civil War become more dim and distant. Its heroes pass on and beyond, but the object for which they gave their lives must forever be preserved. It is, therefore, wise and fitting that the mothers, sisters, daughters and loyal women of the Woman's Relief Corps should take the little ones by the hand, and from the lessons of the past teach them their duty as to the future welfare and happiness of their country. In what more impressive manner can this be done than by saluting the Flag of our Country?—Emma R. Wallace, National President W. R. C.

> "And they fought and conquered on freedom's side,
> With the chief, Columbia's noblest pride."

> "Where the battle's wreck lies thickest,
> And death's brief pang is quickest."

WHAT IS PATRIOTISM.

INSPIRATIONS FROM THE SONS AND DAUGHTERS OF PATRIOTS.

A loyal and unswerving devotion to the flag and the institutions of one's government. It is a zealous love of country, that is neither corrupted nor consumed by mercenary motives, nor blasted nor chilled by adversity, but remains firm even when life is at stake.—John E. Haslacker, W. Va.

The passion which aims to serve one's country, either defending it from invasion or protecting its rights, and maintaining its law and institutions in vigor and purity is the noblest passion that animates man and makes him an honorable and useful citizen.—Grace G. Hunt, Ohio.

That feeling of love and pride that makes us live and dare to die for our country, that seeks to preserve our sacred institutions from harm, and to hand down our inheritance of liberty unsullied to those who succeed us.—T. E. Hickmon, Ark.

Patriotism is the love of our country; it is the passion which aims to serve our country, either in defending it from invasion or protecting its rights and maintaining its laws and institutions in vigor and purity; it is the characteristic of a good citizen, the noblest passion that animates man.—Rhoda Sehl, Iowa.

Devotion to equal rights and justice to all, as a principle of a national government.—Wayland F. Webster, Wis.

The love that makes men leave their dear ones and homes to face the leaden rain of bullets and death in every form that they may defend their loved country from those who wish to destroy it.—Edith M. Haines, Mo.

The grateful reciprocity of paternal protection, and the divine flame of love that burns brightest in adversity and sheds its impartial rays on all who answer to the name of brother; it is the inspiration that creates heroic living, and the aspiration that emulates sacrificial dying.—Georgia A. Martin, Ky.

> 'Tis love for our country, with duty fulfilled,
> 'Tis helping to govern as God has willed:
> 'Tis loyalty shown, maintaining the cause
> Of national honor, and keeping the laws,
> A citizen's glory, a Nation's delight,
> 'Tis serving our country with might and right.
> —Mrs. Josephine Llewellyn, Ill.

That which animates one who is ready, at the first tap of the drum, to lay down everything—lucrative position, comforts of home and society—when his country calls for volunteers for the defense of the Stars and Stripes, without hope of reward.—Andrew J. Grayson, Ind.

The emotion or impulse in man, which, regardless of consequences to himself, impels him to lend his aid to secure the furtherance and execution of all schemes whereby the welfare of his country is most enhanced and the greatest amount of happiness secured to his countrymen.—W. S. Riley, Mo.

That which animates the typical citizen, one whose love of home and country is so great as to influence his every act for their happiness and prosperity, and who freely makes sacrifices of self for that end. —C. W. Colby, Ill.

Loving our country, rejoicing in its prosperity; ever ready to defend it; always true to its best interests.—Minta Lavy, O.

Patriotism means love of country, to be interested in its welfare, and to lend our influence in the direction that will best benefit the people as a whole; to regard our native land above all others, and to be willing to give our lives to its protection if need be.—Carry M. Brown, O.

The absorbing love in the breast of true patriots among mankind; the love that makes them loyal to rulers, gives them courage to bid adieu to all that is dear, face dangers and battles, suffer imprisonment or death, that their country may be preserved and their flag kept floating. —M. M. Kerschner, Ia.

That emotion which fills the heart of man with love for his country. —Hattie L. Hunt, Ohio.

Heartfelt love for one's country and the national flag, emblem of the country. All who are patriotic have respect for and obey its Constiution and laws, if they are righteous laws, and are willing to aid, yes, offer their lives, to protect their country in all just causes.—Adah Bell Bicknell, N. Y.

A love so great and powerful that it subdues all selfish feelings gives us the strength and courage to endure cold, hunger, hardship, suffering, and brave death in every shape for our country.—Christian Simenson, Minn.

To love, honor and obey the just laws of your country, to emulate the deeds of those who fought in her defense, to teach others to do likewise, and, if need be, to give your life for your country.—Florence G. Crossman, R. I.

A love for country is so great that one would sacrifice everything and die rather than betray his country. And if a man has true patriotism he will defend his country whenever the opportunity is offered.—M. Lenna Streeter, Mich.

An intense love for God, truth and country; like a bright and shining light springing from the depths of love in our hearts, as from an everflowing fountain, inextinguishable only as the heartstrings break in death. —Allen Marlin, Kan.

Is that love which causes a man to forsake home, wife, mother, children, and all that is near and dear, and offer his service and life, if need be, for his country.—J. W. Cole, Ky.

Is the sea over which the craft of the government of the United States sails, and where the sailors ever keep the Stars and Stripes floating in the breeze of freedom.—J. O. Silverwood, Kan.

Is the love of one's country; it contains the true meaning of all together; in fact, it is the principle in the character of a man which spurs him on to do or to die for his country.—E. W. Goodlin, Ohio.

The gratitude and sympathy we feel towards great men and loyal women, and the labor of love we bestow on the old soldiers of this, our beloved country.—Mrs. Mary E. Hunt, Ohio.

That love which nerves men to maintain the rights of the people and the country regardless of consequences, as our ancestors and sires have done in days gone by.—Lou M. Staring, Tenn.

To love our country as we should God and humanity.—Mildred N. Baldwin, Ohio.

Is that God-given gift, or faculty, which enables a man to honestly, deeply and sincerely appreciate his country and hold it in sacred remembrance always.—W. C. Horton, N. J.

A love for our country and our country's flag; it is the love for our home, for the spot where we live, were brought up and taught to love from infancy; not the love of another country, but of our own.—Ida M. Koontz, Ind.

Love of God and our country, and the willingness to leave everything that is dear, if need be, to serve, protect, or stand up for our God and our country.—Lillie V. Clark, Ill.

That love and devotion which inspires us to meet nobly and unselfishly any service required of us for our country's welfare. A. Grace, Pa.

That devotion which makes persons willing to render their country a service through love of it, without thought of pecuniary gain.—Theo. Gieszlaman, Ill.

The second brightest jewel in the crown of manhood; the first being love of God.—A. P. Goff, N. Y.

Love for God and home and native land.—Alice Gender, Ohio.

That love which enables one to speak, fight and even dare to die for his country.—Lillian Stormont, Ind.

A true love of country, whether manifested in time of war or peace.—Burt Stone, Ia.

WHAT IS OUR FLAG?

Inspirations from the Sons and Daughters of Patriots.

THE TRIUMPHANT AMERICAN FLAG.

By Supt. Wm. Connell, Fall River, Mass.

(Tune—"Auld Lang Syne.")

The flag that speaks of Bunker Hill,
  Of minute men and gun,
Of Saratoga and Yorktown,—
  Fierce battles fought and won.

CHORUS:

That flag we'll raise upon our school,
  With stars now forty-four;
Triumphant Red, and White, and Blue,
  The flag our fathers bore.

The flag that waved o'er Gettysburg
  On those eventful days;
The flag our boys in blue upheld
  'Mid battle's storm always.
Cho.—That flag we'll raise, etc.

The flag that Lincoln freed from stain,
  By setting bondmen free,—
The flag that can forgive a wrong,—
  Rebellion though it be.
Cho.—That flag we'll raise, etc.

The flag that drew rebellious men
  Into the Union fold,—
The flag that is respected now
  In States both new and old,—
Cho.—That flag we'll raise, etc.

The flag that now waves o'er our homes,
  Protecting weak and strong,—
The flag that vindicates the right,
  And punishes the wrong,—
Cho.—That flag we'll raise, etc.

Through what scenes has our flag not passed? what storms of shot and shell? how many have lived for it? how many have its folds draped in death? how many living and dying have said: "Oh, the flag, the glorious Stars and Stripes!" It is the same old flag inscribed with the dying words of Lawrence: "Don't give up the ship," that was hoisted on Lake Erie on the eve of Perry's great naval victory. What countries has it not visited, the pride of its friends, the terror of its foes! None but tyrants hate it! All who sigh for progress and patriotism love and honor it!—Fannie C. Steele, Mo.

Our glorious flag has led the braves to victory; it has floated over our cradles; let it be our prayer that it float in triumph above our graves. —Walter F. Senor, Texas.

The colors are Union, Peace and Freedom. The white is the celestial whiteness of Heaven; the blue is the sky; the red is the morning light.

Each star is a State, and the stripes are the thirteen Colonies that won their independence.—Geo. W. Burton, Ill.

I have no room for any one who is not willing to vow allegiance to that flag which is powerful enough to shield and protect us in the exercises of civil and religious liberty. Our flag is the symbol of all that makes a home for us.—M. Burlison, Wis.

The red, white and blue—fervency, purity and truth—holds in its meaning to us freedom, and it has been said, "Freedom can never die." Ernest R. Ostrom, Iowa.

Our flag, the stars and stripes! Emblem of freedom, of justice and true American patriotism and loyalty.—Lillian Knight, Minn.

The American flag is symbolic of liberty and union, purity and strength. Let us strive to keep it so; pure, strong and just. May it remain for ages to shed its patriotic influence on all American citizens, and may its luster never grow dim. Let us hope that our Nation is steadily marching forward, onward and upward, and that the sword of combat is forever sheathed in the scabbard of peace. Let us encourage and foster patriotism in our hearts, and strive to awaken it in the hearts of the rising generation, that our flag may ever be supported and defended.—Marie H. Oliver, Iowa.

How our hearts thrill with joy as we behold this beauteous emblem of liberty floating in the air over the school-houses or other public buildings. It tells of many hard fought battles, many soldiers wounded and many homes made desolate, that it might represent America's freedom and proclaim her peace to all nations.—Edith M. Haynes, Mo.

Glorious emblem of the Nation's purity and grace, progress and patriotism; made sacred by the lives sacrificed in the cause of freedom and justice to all. The heart of every true American, as he beholds this victorious banner, thrills with joy and pride that he may stand beneath its folds and say, "God bless our country and our flag."—Ella V. Garton, South Dakota.

The grandest, most beautiful emblem of liberty that floats to the breeze, beneath the ever watchful eye of Almighty God.—G. E. Hounson, Mo.

The flag is the emblem of our country. It is our pride, our companion, our protector.—W. L. Hedges, Wis.

As I read the never dying Declaration of Independence asserting the inalienable rights of man, as I study the Constitution of our Nation giving us the rights of liberty bought with precious blood, as I love my country and my country's flag, the most beautiful and significant emblem ever unfurled to the winds of heaven, with the grandest galaxy of stars that ever shone o'er enlightened men, then I say, palsied be the tongue that would speak a word other than in its praise.—Lutie Fairbanks, Mo.

When we see the flag floating so proudly, it reminds us of something that happened over one hundred years ago, and that was the winning of independence and liberty. Thirteen stripes for the Union now, and forty-five stars for the Union maintained our glorious banner bears.—Arthur L. Hynds, Texas.

The American flag is an emblem of American characteristics in national life; white the emblem of purity, red of valor and blue of justice. It represents everything that is dear to us, and is our emblem of national power and honor.—Carrie Hornell, Mo.

Our flag, that sacred emblem of liberty, under whose folds numberless heroes have nobly fought and bravely perished for their country, should have a place of deep affection in the hearts of every American citizen.—Jas. F. Balls, Mo.

The red, white and blue colors of our flag are symbolic of Divine love, truth, hope and loyalty. Their language is valor, purity and sincerity; they are emblematic of war, peace and justice.—Geo. E. Hunter, Ind.

The Star Spangled Banner, that has had so many historical changes since its birth and will doubtless have many more, is very dear to our country. If the tales it bears in its folds of scenes of sorrow and the triumph it has witnessed could be told, what volumes it would fill. May every boy and girl always revere this brave old flag.—Nella D. Hampson, O.

Our Nation's pride and defense, emblem of unity, liberty and justice, animating the progress of our fair land and winning the admiration of the world.—Flora Dell Ellis, Ind.

May the red, white and blue wave forever peacefully over us.—Lee Berry, Pa.

Old Glory! Starry flag of the free! I pledge my life and service to thee; and so will every true American.—M. Couch, Iowa.

Emblematic of fame, glory and honor; emitting from its starry folds a thousand rays of love, hope and peace to all.—Ora A. Kost, Mich.

>I pledge allegiance to my flag, and
>The Republic for which it stands—
>One Nation indivisible,
>With Liberty and Justice for all.
>
>—Frank Bellamy.

THE LIBERTY BELL.

The bell was made in London; it weighed 2,000 pounds and cost nearly $500.

It has on it the words, "Proclaim liberty throughout all the land and unto all the inhabitants thereof."—Leviticus, xxv, 10.

The bell was cracked when it was brought to this country in 1752, and two men recast it. It was hung in the State House in Philadelphia in 1753.

This was the first bell to ring and tell the people of the signing of the Declaration of Independence, July 4, 1776.

After fifty years more it became so badly cracked that it could not be used. It is still kept in the old State House.

INSPIRATIONS.

We sing of thee to-day, O Bell,
Loud let our tones of music swell!
All o'er the land; let all be free,
And sing, O Bell, to-day of thee.
—Elsie Lowry, Ind., 13 years of age.

Old Liberty Bell, old Liberty Bell!
How did your ring sound out so well?
Your ring was pure and clear.
This makes us love our country dear.
—Emil Camphausen, Ind., 14 years of age.

> We welcome this bell for its teachings alone,
> This bell so true and so grand—
> It stands for Liberty, Justice and Right,
> The glory and pride of the land.
>
> —Samuel K. Selig, Ind., 12 year of age.

> What though 'tis voiced weak and low—
> We know 'twas once a joyous swell.
> And must we never, never know
> The sound of thy voice, and its spell?
>
> —Marie Page, Ind., 13 years of age.

IMPORTANT ANNIVERSARIES AND NOTABLE PATRIOTIC EVENTS IN THE HISTORY OF OUR COUNTRY.

JANUARY.

"Oh, dawn of a fair New Year, content will we stand looking towards the sunlight of this glad new month, leaving God to order all our ways. What lies beyond is His to know; our part to patiently wait His will, and trust in Him through good or ill, our faces ever towards the East—the sunrise city of the soul."

New Year's day.

I wish you not only a happy New Year, but a happy eternity.—W. S. Plummer.

President Lincoln's Emancipation Proclamation issued 1st, 1863.

Charles Sumner, born 6th, 1811; died March 11th, 1874.

General Israel Putnam, born 7th, 1718.

> "Up with the shout! for Putnam comes, upon his reeking bay,
> With bloody spur and foaming bit, in haste to join the fray."

Battle New Orleans, 8th, 1815.

General G. K. Warren, born 8th, 1830; died August 8th, 1882.

> "To arms! to arms, they cry:
> Defend the flag or die!
> To arms! as in the year
> When heroes saw the field of battle nigh."

> Another hand thy sword shall wield,
> Another hand the standard wave,
> Till from the trumpet's mouth is peal'd
> The blast of triumph o'er the grave.
>
> —Bryant.

Alexander Hamilton, born 11th, 1757; died July 12th, 1804.

He smote the rock of the national resources, and abundant streams of revenue gushed forth. He touched the dead corpse of Public Credit, and it sprung upon its feet.—Daniel Webster.

Thos. J. Edison, born 11th, 1847.

Bayard Taylor, born 11th, 1825.

John Hancock, born 12th, 1737.

He said: "Burn Boston! and make John Hancock a beggar if the public good requires it."

Siege of Fort Fisher, N. C., 13th to 15th, 1865.

General Judson Kilpatrick, born 14th, 1836; died December 4th, 1881.
A true patriot, genial, generous and beloved.
General Henry W. Halleck, born 16th, 1815; died 9th, 1872.
Benjamin Franklin, born 17th, 1706; died April 17th, 1790.
"We must all hang together, or we will all hang separately."
"He snatched the lightning from the sky, and the scepter from the tyrants."
"Dost thou love life? Then do not squander time, for that is the stuff life is made of."
Daniel Webster, born 18th, 1782; died October 24th, 1852.
"One country, one Constitution, one destiny."
Robert Morris, born 20th, 1734.
Without the assistance of Robert Morris, of Philadelphia, even Washington could not have saved the country.—Fiske.
Congress charters the Bank of North America, 20th, 1781.
I am determined that the bank shall be well supported till it can support itself, then it will support us.—Robert Morris.
General John C. Fremont, born 21st, 1813; died July 13th, 1890.
A zealous man; an upright citizen.
Gen. Robert Sanford Foster, born Jan. 27, 1834.
An honorable and upright patriotic citizen; a brave and fearless soldier, who did his whole duty to his country and flag, and never knew defeat in battle.

> When wasteful war shall statues overturn,
> And broils root out the work of masonry,
> Nor Mars his sword nor wars quick fire
> The living record of his memory shall burn.
> —Shakespeare.

FEBRUARY.

"How soft is the step of this royal newcomer; for, oh, underneath him lie folded buds and blossoms, and the time is not yet for their glad awakening. Speak gently, O King February! for they are sleeping but lightly, and the bosom of Mother Earth shall cradle them only a little longer."
Provincial Congress met in Philadelphia 1st, 1775.
"Our own, our country's honor, calls upon us for a vigorous and manly exertion."
Slavery abolished, 1st, 1865.
James Otis, born 5th, 1725.
He spoke, and into every heart his words carried new strength and courage.—Bryant.
American Independence recognized by France, 6th, 1778.
General Wm. T. Sherman, born 8, 1820; died 14, 1891.
A true hero of the Union army.

> "For desperate fighting in the war
> Thou wert a hero to the end,
> Bearing the heat, the brunt, the scar,
> Our fair country to defend."

General John A. Logan, born 9th, 1826; died December 26th, 1886.
A brave man, a faithful, patriotic citizen.
Abraham Lincoln, born February 12th, 1809.
"With malice towards none, with charity for all, with firmness in the right as God gives us to see the right."

'Tis Lincoln's Day.
All nature clothed in purest white
  Pays homage to the spotless soul
That purged the land of slav'ry's blight
  And paid a nation's final toll.
Blazed bright in Fame's undying scroll
  His name must live for aye and aye
And lead the Martyr's Honor roll—
             'Tis Lincoln's Day.

Count Kosciusko, born 12th, 1746; died October 15th, 1817.

Hope for a season bade the world farewell,
And Freedom shrieked when Kosciusko fell.
                              —Campbell.

General John A. Rawlings, born 13th, 1831; died 9th, 1869.
Gen. W. S. Hancock, born 14th, 1824; died 9th, 1886.
St. Valentine's Day, 14th.

"Love with all your heart and soul,
  Love with eye and ear and touch;
That's the moral of the whole,
  You can never love too much."

Battle of Fort Donelson, 15th and 16th, 1862.
General John E. Wool, born 20th, 1784; died November 10th, 1869.
General William Prescott, born 20th, 1726.

Up with the pine-tree banner!
  Our gallant Prescott stands
Amid the plunging shell and shot,
  And plants it with his hands.
                              —F. S. Cozzens.

James Russell Lowell, born 22nd, 1819; died August 12th, 1891.

"Once to every man and nation comes a moment to decide.
In the strife of Truth with Falsehood, for the good or evil side."

When a deed is done for freedom, through the broad earth's breast
Runs a thrill of joy prophetic, trembling on from east to west.
                              —Lowell.

Battle Buena Vista, Mexico, 22nd to 23rd, 1847.
Washington's birthday (22nd, 1732). National holiday.

Yes—one—the first, the last, the best,
  The Cincinnatus of the West,
    Whom envy dare not hate;
Bequeathed the name of Washington
  To make men blush, there was but one.
                              —Lord Byron.

Charles C. Pinkney, born 25th, 1706.
"Millions for defense, sir, but not one cent for tribute."

Henry Wadsworth Longfellow, born 27th, 1807; died March 24th, 1882.

"Not marble, nor the gilded monuments
  Of princes, shall outlive his beautiful rhymes;
But he shall shine more bright in these contents
  Than unswept Stone besmeared with filthy time."

Francis Marion, born 1732; died 27th, 1795. "The Swamp Fox."

> "A moment in the British camp,
> A moment—and away
> Back to the pathless forest
> Before the break of day."

> "Their hearts are all with Marion,
> For Marion their prayers."

Colonel William Washington, born 28th, 1752.

> "To foes, how stern a foe was he,
> And to the valiant and the free
> How brave a chief!"

MARCH.

"Another spring has dawned; and down the avenue of Time our winter has silently stolen away. Now the furry catkins begin to unfold their downy buds, and early flowers are peeping from the leafy mould and swelling into beauty and fragrance. The maple's heart pours out its nectar, and the honied drops gush forth at every outlet."

Inauguration Day, 4th.

"Long live the good men who are entrusted with our public welfare; and may the memory of those who have been called to their reward ever dwell in our hearts."

> "Columbia, Columbia to glory arise,
> The queen of the world and the child of the skies."
> —Timothy Dwight.

General Pulaski, born 4th, 1748; died October 11th, 1779.

General Philip H. Sheridan, born 6th, 1831; died February 14th, 1893.

> Blow bugler, soft thy bugles blow—
> Weep every heart that loved him so,
> And children tell in friendly clan
> Of Winchester and Sheridan.
> The Francis Marion of the day
> O'er hills and plains away, away—
> While pale he rests in glory won,
> On thy green slope, sweet Arlington.
> —Mary Baird Finch.

On the 8th, 1862, United States war vessels Congress and Cumberland sunk by the rebel gun boat, Merrimac.

9th, 1862, battle between the Monitor and Merrimac. "The Monitor went smack into the Merrimac and on her sides played Yankee Doodle Dandy, Oh."

Joseph Trumbull, Commissary General of the Continental Army, born 11th, 1737.

> And ne'er shall the sons of Columbia be slaves,
> While the earth bears a plant, or the sea rolls its waves.

Admiral John L Worden., commander of the Monitor, born 12, 1818, died Oct. 18, 1897.
"The love of liberty with life is given,
And life itself the inferior gift of Heaven."

Gen. John Pope, born 16, 1823, died Sept. 23, 1892.

Andrew Jackson, born 15, 1767. "Old Hickory."
"Our Federal Union! it must be preserved."

Governor Jonathan Trumbull, born 26, 1740. "Brother Jonathan."
"Hands that the rod of empire might have swayed."
—Gray.

APRIL.

"This is our day. Look how the world brightens for it is now the beginning of a happy time to come! Dear heart, let us be glad today, and let us look trustingly on and beyond us, knowing that God has in store many folded buds for love and happiness that all shall awaken in His sunlight and bloom for us."

Arbor month. Tree planting; also last week in October and first week in November observed.

Washington Irving, born 3rd, 1783; died Nov. 28th, 1859. One of America's great historians.

Surrender of Gen. Robert E. Lee and the Southern Confederacy at Appomattox, Va., 9th, 1865. Close of the War of the Rebellion.

Fort Sumter fired upon by rebels 12th and 13th, 1861. Commencement of the War of the Rebellion.

Henry Clay born 12, 1777, died July 29, 1852.
"His heart and hand were ever ready
To do a generous deed,
His kindness true and steady
To all who stood in need."

"I have heard something said about allegiance to the South. I know no South, no North, no East, no West, to which I owe allegiance."

Thomas Jefferson born 13, 1743.
Jefferson, with those large, fair ideas of freedom and equality so dear to men.
"For friend or foe when in distress,
He had sympathy and tears,
And with his gentle tenderness
Would calm and soothe their fears."

Stars and Stripes replaced over Fort Sumter, 14th, 1865.

"Though changes may the world appall,
Though crown may break and thrones may fall,
Our banner may survive them all
And ever live in story;
The rainbow of a rescued land,
Where freemen brave together stand,
Where truth and courage hand in hand
Floats proudly here, Old Glory!"
—P. A. Gifford.

Battle Cerro Gordo, Mexico, 17 and 18, 1847.
First battle of the Revolution at Lexington, 19, 1775.
There the first British blood was shed—there the first British graves were dug.

Battle at Concord, 19th, 1775.
>By the rude bridge that arched the flood,
>Their flags to April breeze unfurled,
>There once the embattled farmers stood
>And fired the shot heard round the world.
>—Emerson.

Siege of Boston begun, 20th, 1775.
>There might our ringing cheer
>Beleaguered Boston hear,
>Tell how we sped.

Battle San Jacinto, Texas, 21th, 1847.

Governor Trumbull born 24th, 1750.
>"He above the rest,
>In shape and gesture proudly eminent,
>Stood like a statue."

MAY.

"And now it is May Day; the lilacs are nodding their purple and white plumes, and the sweet-breathed cherry blossoms are hourly opening into new white stars. In full symmetrical globes of bloom stands the stately gelder rose, lifting her crown of purity up into the blue sky,—and all the earth rejoices and praises God."

Battle of Chancellorsville, Va., 1st to 4th, 1863.
>It was twilight hour on the second of May,
>The flowers looked up from the sod;
>And the nesting of birds in the hush of the day
>Sang matins of praises to God.
>But the sun had spread over valley and hill
>A mantle of blood on the grim battlefield;
>None more do we honor, whose names shall live still,
>Than these martyred heroes at Chancellorsville.
>—Libbie C. Baer.

Treaty of alliance between France and the United States, 3rd, 1778.
May the friendship of the two Republics be commensurate with their existence—George Washington.

Horace Mann, born 4, 1776.
Battle Palo Alto, Mexico 8th, 1846.

Gen. John Stark died 8th, 1822.
"There they are boys! We beat them today, or Mollie Stark's a widow."

John Brown, born 9th, 1800; died December 2nd, 1859.
"He grew up a religious and manly person, in severe poverty; a fair specimen of the best stock of New England; having that force of thought and that sense of right which are the warp and woof of greatness."—Emerson.

Ethan Allen captured Ticonderoga 10th, 1776.
"In the name of the Great Jehovah and the Continental Congress."

Battle Champion Hill, Miss., 16th, 1863.

Israel Putnam died 19th, 1790.
"He dared to lead where any dared to follow."

Gen. A. E. Burnside, born 23rd, 1824, died Sept. 13th, 1881.

First telegraph message 24th, 1844.

Ralph Waldo Emerson, born 25th, 1803, died April 27th, 1882.
>When the Church is social worth:
>When the State House is the hearth;
>Then the perfect state is come,
>The Republican at home."
>
>—Emerson.

>"So nigh is grandeur to our dust,
>So near is God to man,
>When Duty whispers low, 'Thou must,'
>The youth replies, 'can.'"
>
>—Emerson.

General Nathaniel Greene, born 27th, 1742, died June 19th, 1786.
>Nurtured in peril, lo! the peril came,
>To lead him on from field to field—to fame.

"My diplomacy is in the mouth of my cannon."

Patrick Henry, born 29th, 1736, died June 6th, 1799.
"I know not what course others may take; but as for me, give me liberty, or give me death."
>One of the few—the immortal names
>That were not born to die.
>
>—Halleck.

Battle of Corinth, Miss., 30th, 1862.

Memorial Day, 30th.
"The broken ranks shall once more bend above their comrades' graves and all lay their precious offerings there, but sweeter than the flowers they bring will be the heart-felt, silent tear that springs unbidden to the eye. Sleep well, O brave and noble ones."

Walt Whitman born 31st, 1819, died March 26, 1892.
We have seen the alacrity with which the American-born populace, the peaceblest and most good-natured race in the world, and the most personally independent and intelligent, and the least fitted to submit to the irksomeness and exasperation of regimental discipline, sprang, at the first tap of the drum, to arms—not for gain, nor even glory, nor to repel invasion—but for an emblem, a mere abstraction—for the life, the safety of the flag.—Walt Whitman.

JUNE.

"Oh, lovely June now beautifies the ground, and smiles on earth and sky. There is no nook so deeply hidden but feels the warmth of her welcome presence, and no brook or stream too small to reflect her image.

O, rare sweet June, our hearts grow lighter because of your coming; we lift grateful hearts to Heaven that earth is made so wondrous fair to us."

Gen. Phil Kearney, born 2nd, 1815, killed in the battle of Chantilly, Va., Sept. 1st, 1862.
> "Thou hast gone, old soldier, true and brave,
> Above the stars in mystic lands to dwell.
> Farewell! thou hast passed beyond the grave,
> Farewell, dear Comrade, a long farewell."

Gen. Benjamin F. Butler's famous Flag Order No. 10, 5th, 1862.

Wm. B. Mumford, a citizen of New Orleans, before a military commission, having been convicted of treason, in tearing down the United States flag from a public building of the United States, for the purpose of inciting other evil-minded persons to further resistance to the laws and arms of the United States, after said flag was placed there by Commodore (flag officer) Farragut, of the United States navy.

"It is ordered that he be executed according to the sentence of the said military commission, on Saturday, June 7th, inst., between the hours of eight a. m., and twelve m., under the direction of the provost-marshal of the district of New Orleans; and for so doing this shall be his sufficient warrant."

Gen. Alfred Pleasanton born 7th, 1824.

"In case Congress should think it necessary for the safety of the United Colonies to declare their independence of Great Britain, the inhabitants with their lives and their fortunes will most cheerfully support the measure."—American Press 8th, 1776.

John Howard Payne, author of "Home, Sweet Home," born 9th, 1792, died April 10th, 1852.
> "An exile from home, splendor dazzles in vain
> Oh, give me my lowly thatched cottage again;
> The birds singing gaily, that come at my call;
> Give me them, and that peace of mind, dearer than all."

Nathan Hale resigned his life a sacrifice to his country's liberty; born 9th, 1755, died Sept. 22nd, 1776.

"Who would not be that youth? What pity 'tis that we can die but once to save our country."

"I only regret that I have but one life to lose for my country," were the last words uttered by the young patriot.

Battle between the Kearsarge and Alabama, 10th, 1864.

Declaration of Independence drafted 11th, 1776.

Gen. Winfield Scott born 13th, 1817, died May 29th, 1886.

Flag Day—Stars and Stripes adopted 14th, 1777.

The day should be celebrated by unfurling the flag over every school, and over public and private buildings with appropriate exercises.

> A song for our banner! The watchword recall
> Which gave the Republic her station:
> "United we stand, divided we fall."
> It made and preserves us a nation."
>   —George C. Morris.

> "Then let the starry banner wave;
> Let songs o'er the nation ring,
> To hail the flag that freemen gave—
> A costly, bright and sacred thing—
> Till stars shall crowd upon the field,
> Undimmed with aught of error's night,
> Whose bliss shall be the earth revealed,
> That freedom is Eternal right!"
>   —William Oland Bourne.

Gen. Robert Anderson, "Hero of Fort Sumter," born 14th, 1805, died Oct. 27th, 1871.

Washington appointed Commander-in-Chief of the Continental Army 15th, 1775.

> "And immortal Washington
> Led Columbia's patriots on
> Till the glorious prize was won—
> Peace and Liberty."

Battle of Bunker Hill 17th, 1775.

> "What though the day to us was lost, upon the deathless page
> The everlasting charter stands, for every land and age."

Admiral George Brown, born 19th, 1835.
A typical patriotic American citizen, a loyal sailor who served his country and flag with distinguished honors, upholding them right or wrong.

Gen. Abner Doubleday born 26th, 1819, died Jan. 28th, 1893.

Battle of Monmouth, N. J., 28th, 1778.

JULY.

"The year is half gone, and we stand today looking into the face of July, wondering what she has in store for us. The passing days have had their bitter and sweet. Trials or sorrows are hardest while we live them; joys are sweetest when they are gone. But let us thank God for both."

Battle of Malvern Hill 1st, 1862. The last of the seven days' battles.

Battle of Gettysburg 1st to 3rd, 1863.

Independence Day, 4th, 1776. National Holiday.

Signing the Declaration of Independence, 4th, 1776.
This nation, under God, shall have a new birth of freedom, that government of the people, by the people, and for the people, shall not perish from the earth.—Abraham Lincoln.

The generations of men shall come and go, the greatness shall be forgotten today, and the glories of this noon shall vanish before tomorrow's sun; but America shall not perish, but endure while the spirit of our fathers animates their sons.—Henry Armitt Brown.

Surrender of Vicksburg, Miss., 4th, 1863.

Admiral David G. Farragut born 5th, 1801, died Aug. 14th, 1870.
Here's one whose fearless courage never failed in fight,
Who guarded with zeal our country's flag, our freedom and our right.

St. Clair abandoned Ticonderoga 5th, 1777.
Of the loss of Ticonderoga wrote John Adams—"We shall never be able to defend a post till we shoot a general."

Paul Jones born 6th, 1747, died July 18th, 1792.
> The spirit of our Yankee tars was stronger than their ships,
> You know from Fame's own lips,

Victory of Paul Jones off the coast of England, 1779.

> May the service united ne'er sever,
> But they to the colors prove true;
> The army and navy for ever:
> Three cheers for the red, white, and blue!

And the name of John Paul Jones and the Bonhomme Richard will go down the annals of time forever.

On the 9th, 1776, the populace of New York tore down the leaden statue of George III, which was cast into forty thousand bullets by patriotic women.—Irving.

So, said a contemporary writer, "They had melted Majesty hurled at them."

Gen. David Hunter, born 21st, 1802, died Feb. 2nd, 1886.

Gen. Jno. A. Dix, born 24th, 1798, died April 21st, 1879.

"If any one attempts to haul down the American Flag shoot him on the spot."

> "Our flag is the symbol of power,
> The emblem of union and truth;
> It waves o'er the land of the free,
> As fair as the visions of youth.
> It never shall sink in disgrace
> While a true heart remains in our land;
> We will leave to our children that flag
> As pure as it came to our hand."
>
> —Gilbert Nash.

Gen. George H. Thomas, "The Rock of Chickamauga," born 31st, 1816, died March 28, 1890.

AUGUST.

"All silent she steals in among us,—quiet, dreamy August, following close on the footsteps of daisy-crowned July. The poppy blazes in the sunshine, the grain fields are ripening into golden splendor, and the butterflies and humming birds seemed to have gathered the gorgeousness of nature's lovliest hues and imprisoned them within their folded wings."

Declaration of Independence signed by representatives of the Thirteen States, 2nd, 1776.

"Liberty and union, one and inseparable, now and forever."

2nd, 1777, Stars and Stripes were unfurled for the first time on a fort.

Oliver Perry Morton (war governor of Indiana) born 4th, 1823, died Nov. 1st, 1877.

"He loved his country's good, with a respect more tender, more holy and profound, than his own life."

Naval battle and siege of Mobile Bay, Ala., 5th to 23rd, 1864.

Gen. Lovel H. Rousseau, born 4th, 1818, died Jan. 7, 1869.

Gen. Nelson A. Miles, born 8th, 1839.

General Andrew Pickens died 17th, 1817.

> Whose valiant sword and stout right arm,
> With many a timely blow,
> Have wrought new glory for its stars,
> And crushed the haughty foe.

Battles in front of Petersburg and Weldon Railroad, Va., 18th to 25th, 1864.

Battle Cherusbusco, Mexico, 20th, 1847.

Mary, mother of Washington, died 25th, 1789.

> A perfect woman, nobly planned,
> To warn, to comfort, to command,
> And yet a spirit still and bright,
> With something of an angel light.

Washington's address before the battle of Long Island 27th, 1776:
"Let us then rely on the goodness of our cause and the aid of the Supreme Being, in whose hands victory is, to animate and encourage us to great and noble action."

John Stark, born 28th, 1728.
>There sounds not to the trump of fame
>The echo of a nobler name.

Oliver Wendell Holmes, born 29th, 1809, died Oct. 7th, 1894.
>His life was gentle; the elements
>So mixed in him that nature
>Might stand up and say to
>All the world, This was a man.
>—Shakespeare.

The great French squadron arrived off Yorktown, 31st, 1781.
>Then rang the cheer that all the shores repeat,
>Re-echoing o'er the sea.

SEPTEMBER.

"Like an oriental princess comes the beautiful maid September. All silently she buries her shapely feet among the grasses, and trails her stately garments down the wooden aisles, and the woodland echoes whisper to each other, 'Behold, September is here!' Our fair, sweet Summer has flown, but lo, in her stead September walks among us clothed in all the regal splendor of autumnal colors."

First Monday "Labor Day."

Final treaty of peace with Great Britain signed, 3rd, 1783.

"Blessed with victory and peace, may the Heaven-rescued land praise the Power that hath made and preserved us a nation."

Continental Congress first session at Philadelphia, Pa., 5th, 1774.

Removed to Washington, D. C., 1801.

Gen. Wm. S. Rosecrans, born 6th, 1819, a devout Christian soldier and loyal citizen.

Gen, Marquis de Lafayette, born 6th, 1757, died May 20, 1834.
>One in our faith, and one our longing
>To make the world within our reach
>Somewhat the better for our living,
>And gladder for our human speech.
>—Whittier.

>And soon to the flag from the Gallic shore
>Came a noble youth the rough sea o'er;
>And others from thence his steps pursued,
>Their hearts with freedom's love imbued.

First battle under the Stars and Stripes 11th, 1777.

Gen. John Sedgwick, born 13th, 1813, killed at Spottsylvania, Va.,

Birth of our National Hymn, "Star Spangled Banner," 14th, 1818.

Perry's victory on Lake Erie, 10th, 1813.

Mexico surrendered 14th, 1847.

Battle of Chapultepec, Mexico, 13th, 1847.

Battle of South Mountain 14th, 1862.

Adoption United States Constitution 17th, 1787.

Battle of Monterey, Mexico, 21st to 23rd, 1846.

Gen. John F. Reynolds, born 20th, 1820, killed at the battle of Gettysburg, 1st, 1863.

Emancipation Day Proclamation 22nd, 1862.

Lieut. Stafford's heroic act in saving the Stars and Stripes on the Bor Homme Richard 23rd, 1779.

The Stars and Stripes entwined for the first time with the French flag in friendly communion 25th, 1794.

Samuel Adams, "Father of the American Revolution," born 27th, 1722. Probably no other man did as much as he to bring about the Declaration of Independence.—Appleton.

Gen. John M. Schofield, born 29th, 1831.

Gen. Samuel P. Heintzelman, born 30th, 1805, died May 1st, 1880.

OCTOBER.

"October, the month of joy, and fruitfulness. The autumn leaves burn red and gold, as if enkindled one by one by nature's warm and cheery fires to light the footsteps of the year. The season wings its onward flight; the year is running fast its course, but ere it dies, behold how bright, how beautiful, how glorious its orient hues!"

Gen. E. O. C. Ord, born 1st, 1818, died July 22nd, 1883.

Jonathan Edwards, born 5th, 1703.
>
> And he the good man's shield and shade,
> To whom all hearts their homage paid,
> As virtue's son.

A terrific assault on Savannah, 9th, 1779. French and Americans repulsed.

Sergeant Jasper mortally wounded while placing the flag on the redoubt.
> How curious that a few yards of bunting
> Should have so great a charm!

Discovery of America 12th, 1492.

Noah Webster, born 16th, 1758.
> Aid the dawning tongue and pen;
> Aid it, hopes of honest men;
> Aid it, paper; aid it, type;
> Aid it, for the hour is ripe.

Gen. Burgoyne's surrender 17th, 1777.

Surrender of Cornwallis and the British Army at Yorktown, Va., 19, 1781.

Battle of Cedar Creek, Va., (Sheridan's Ride) 19th, 1864.

Daniel E. Sickles, born 30th, 1822.

"Old Ironside," launched 21st, 1797. Built by contributions of the patriotic women of Boston, Mass.:
> "O, better that her shattered hulk,
> Should sink beneath the waves;
> Her thunder shook the mighty deep,
> And there should be her grave;
> Nail to the mast her holy flag,
> Set every thread-bare sail,
> And give her to the God of Storms
> The lightning and the gale."

Battle of White Plains, New York, 28th, 1776.
> Yet though destruction sweep these lovely plains,
> Rise, fellow-men, our country still remains.
> —Campbell.

NOVEMBER.

"November! her stone the topaz; her motto fidelity. The warm, rich colors of the topaz are lighting the dawn of November, and all her sunsets will wear their soft amber glow. Let us take the motto as our own, and be faithful and true in all things."

Gen. Godfrey Weitzel, born 1st, 1831, died March 19, 1884.
Washington's farewell address to the American Army 2nd, 1783.
"The name of America must always exalt the just pride of patriotism."—Washington.
William Cullen Bryant, born 3rd, 1794, died June 12, 1878.
Gen. Benjamin F. Butler, born 5th, 1818, died Jan. 1st, 1893.
Battle of Tippecanoe, Indiana, 7th, 1811.
Gen. O. O. Howard, born 8th, 1830.
A noble soldier; a lifelong Christian.
First Stars and Stripes raised in Alaska, 8th, 1867.
Elijah P. Lovejoy, born 9th, 1802.
Gen. Alfred H. Terry, born 13th, 1814, died Oct. 31st, 1879.
Gen. J. B. McPherson, born 14th, 1828, killed in battle July 22nd, 1864.
 "Full of hope and manly trust,
  Like those who fell in battle here."
 —Bryant.
Gen. Joe Hooker, born 13th, 1814, died Oct. 31st, 1879.
A braver soldier never fought for his country and flag.
Col. Geo. W. Meikel, born 14, 1837; killed in battle, Sept. 10, 1864.
Gen. Philip Schuyler died 18th, 1804.
 "Patient of toil, serene amidst alarms,
  Inflexible in faith, invincible in arms."
North Carolina ratified the Constitution of the United States 21st, 1789.
 "So acted men
  Like patriots then,
  One hundred years ago."
Wendell Phillips, born 29th, 1811.
"What the Puritans gave the world was not thought, but action."
Battle-Ship Maine, launched November 18, 1890. Destroyed in Havana harbor through Spanish intrigue and treachery February 15, 1898. Commemorate the day with memorial service sacred to the memory of the 253 brave officers and men who sacrificed their lives for their country and flag.
Last Thursday in the month is Thanksgiving Day.
"The thankful heart is full of gratitude at all seasons of the year, but joyfully sets apart one royal day in which to be especially thankful. As the Sabbath is the crown of the week, so is Thanksgiving Day the crown of the year in which jewels of praise shine with brightest lustre."

DECEMBER.

"And now across the face of Time a shadow falls. We greet the twelfth month drawing near and cry, 'You come too soon; our year's good work is not half done.'"

Siege of Nashville, Tenn., 1st to 14th, 1864.
Gen. Geo. B. McClellan, born 3rd, 1826, died Oct. 29th, 1885.
Gen. Geo. A. Custer, born 5th, 1839, killed at battle of Little Big Horn, June 25th, 1876.
A martyr to his country.
Delaware ratified the Constitution of the United States, 6th, 1787.
 "Be just, be brave! and let thy name
  Henceforth Columbia's be.
  And wear the oaken wreath of fame,
  The wreath of Liberty.

William Lloyd Garrison, born 10th, 1805, died May 24th, 1879.
"I will be as harsh as truth and as uncompromising as justice."

Pennsylvania ratified the Constitution of the United States 12th, 1787.
>Thrilling up from each valley,
>Flung down from each height,
>Our Country and Liberty!
>God for the right.

George Washington died December 14th, 1799.
>How needless to him a tomb to raise,
>Whose fame must live to the end of days!
>On a people's hearts, not on senseless stone,
>Is engraven the name of Washington.
>>—Amelia Opie.

John Greenleaf Whittier, born 17th, 1807, died Sept. 7th, 1888.
>"Blessings on the little man,
>Barefoot boy, with cheeks of tan!
>With thy turned-up pantaloons,
>And thy merry whistled tunes;
>With thy red lips redder still,
>Kissed by strawberries on the hill;
>With the sunshine on thy face,
>Through thy torn brain's jaunty grace;
>From my heart I give thee joy—
>I was once a barefoot boy!"

New Jersey ratified the Constitution of the United States 18th, 1787.
>Sail on, O Ship of State!
>Sail on, O Union, strong and great!
>Humanity with all its fears,
>With all the hopes of future years,
>Is hanging breathless on thy fate.
>>—Longfellow.

Landing of the Pilgrims Forefathers Day 22nd, 1761.
>"O earth, O heart, be glad on this glad morn!
>God is with man! Life, life to us is born!"
>>—Lucy Larcom.

Christmas Day, 25th.
A happy greeting! Hail the day of all glad days that bless the year! Oh, may the peace of Christmas-tide be yours in heart and home today, and may a song of praise ascend from happy earth to Heaven above, for this, the sweetest gift of all—the gift of Christ, the Son of God, the King and Saviour of the World! Bright be your hearthstone, glad your heart, and may the song the angels sang of "Peace on Earth, Good-will to men," find echo in your soul today. A merry Christmas-tide be yours.
—Ida Scott Taylor.

Battle of Trenton, N. J., 26th, 1776.
>"And then arose a mighty shout,
>That might have waked the dead,
>'Hurrah! they run—the field is won;
>Hurrah! the foe is fled.'"

Battle of Vicksburg, Miss., 28th and 29th, 1862.

Gen. George G. Meade, born 31st, 1815, died Nov. 6, 1872.
An American nobleman, a faithful Christian soldier.

Presidents of the United States
from 1789 to 1897.

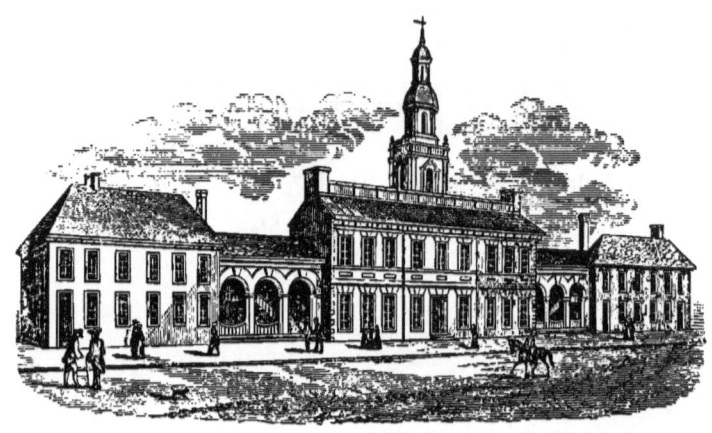

THE BIRTHPLACE OF INDEPENDENCE.

INDEPENDENCE HALL, PHILADELPHIA,

In which the Declaration of Independence was signed by fifty-six representatives of the States, July 4, 1776.

The building was—
  Commenced, 1732.
  Completed, 1741.
  Occupied as "The State House," October, 1735.
  Tower built, 1750.

In this old building was the scene of almost all the civil events of the revolution.

FIRST PRESIDENT, 1789-1797.

GEORGE WASHINGTON

Was born at Bridge Creek, in Westmoreland County, Va., Friday, Feb. 22, 1732. His ancestry was English. He never entered college. His earliest years were spent at Mt. Vernon, Va. He spent three years—from 1748 to 1751—in the survey of large territories in Virginia. In 1751 he was appointed Adjutant-General of the provincial troops, with rank of Major. In 1754 he commanded a regiment against the French; about this time he received the rank of Colonel. In 1759 he married Mrs. Martha Custis, and retired to his estates. For some years he was a member of the Virginia Assembly, and in 1774 took up the cause of the colonists, becoming a member of the Continental Congress. In 1775 he was made Commander-in-Chief of the armies. When independence was achieved, he retired to his estate at Mt. Vernon. He was inaugurated President at New York, April 30, 1789; re-elected 1792. Died at Mt. Vernon, Saturday, December 14, 1799.

John Adams

SECOND PRESIDENT, 1797-1801.

JOHN ADAMS

Was of Puritan descent. Born at Braintree, Massachusetts, Wednesday, October 30, 1735. He taught school for two years, while studying law. In 1770 he was one of the selectmen in the Boston Convention to protest against British imposts on tea, glass, etc. In 1773 he was a member of the Council of State. In 1774 he was one of the delegates to the first Continental Congress, which met at Philadelphia; he advocated the Declaration of Independence, and was pronounced by Jefferson the ablest champion of independence on the floor of the House. In 1780 he was sent as Minister to Holland. In 1782 he negotiated, with others, the Treaty of Peace with England. In 1785 he went as the first Ambassador from the United States to that nation. From 1789 to 1797 was Vice President under Washington. He became President 1797. His death occurred at Quincy, Mass., Tuesday, July 4, 1826.

THIRD PRESIDENT, 1801-1809.

THOMAS JEFFERSON

Was born at Shadwell, Virginia, Tuesday, April 13, 1743. He studied at William and Mary College, and was a member of the first Virginia Convention which met independently of British authority. The original draft of the Declaration of Independence was his work. He was a warm advocate of the abolition of slavery. He was elected Governor of Virginia in 1779. Was sent to Paris to negotiate treaties of commerce with several European powers. In 1789 he was chosen Secretary of State, and served till the close of 1793. Three years later he was chosen Vice President under Adams. In 1800 there was a tie vote for President between Jefferson and Aaron Burr. Jefferson was selected by the House of Representatives. He was re-elected in 1805. Louisiana was acquired by purchase from the French during Jefferson's presidency. By a strange coincidence he died, Tuesday, July 4, 1826, at Monticello, Va., on the same day and year that ex-President John Adams died at Quincy, Mass.

FOURTH PRESIDENT, 1809-1817.

JAMES MADISON

Was born at Port Conway, King George County, Virginia, Friday 16, 1751. He graduated at Princeton College, N. J., in 1771, and afterwards studied law and practiced at the bar; but gave up the profession for politics when the struggle of independence began. In 1776 he became a member of the Virginia Convention: and in 1779 a member of the Federal Congress. He was a member of the Convention of 1787, which met at Philadelphia to form the Constitution. He became a member of the United States Congress in 1789, and united with the Republicans in opposition to the Administration. He was an advocate against Federal encroachment on the rights of States. In 1808 he was elected President. He endeavored in vain to avert the war with England, which was declared in 1812, and which continued for two years. He was re-elected President in 1812, and died at Montpelier, Va., Tuesday, June 28, 1836.

FIFTH PRESIDENT, 1817-1825.

JAMES MONROE

Was born in Westmoreland County, Virginia, Friday, April 28, 1758. He entered the army as a volunteer at the age of eighteen, and was present at several battles. He was wounded at the battle of Trenton. He was educated at William and Mary College, and later studied law. In 1782 he was elected to the Assembly of Virginia, and in 1783 was elected to the General Congress. In 1788 he was one of the Virginia Convention, where he opposed the Constitution, fearing the encroachments of the Federal Government. For two years, from 1794, he was Minister to France. He was for three years Governor of Virginia (1799-1802). In 1803 he was again sent to France to aid in the purchase of Louisiana. He was made Secretary of State in 1811, though just elected Governor of Virginia. In 1816 he was elected President, and was re-elected in 1820. He promulgated what is known as the "Monroe Doctrine," or the policy of non-interference between the United States and the nations of the old world. His death occurred in New York City, N. Y., Monday, July 4, 1831.

SIXTH PRESIDENT, 1825-1829.

JOHN QUINCY ADAMS

Was born at Braintree, Mass., Saturday, July 11, 1767, and was the eldest son of the second President of the United States. He enjoyed rare educational advantages. Accompanying his father to Paris in 1778, he attended school there. Later on he pursued his studies at the University of Leyden. He entered Harvard College in 1786, and graduated from it in 1788. He was admitted to the bar in 1791, and began practice in Boston. He was sent as Minister to Holland in 1794, and in 1797 as Minister to Berlin. In 1803 he was elected United States Senator. He was for a time professor of rhetoric at Harvard. Having a misunderstanding with the Federalists, he became connected with the Coalition party. In 1809 he was appointed Minister to Russia, and was made Secretary of State in 1817. He was elected President in 1824. In 1831 he went to Congress, and served there for seventeen years. His death occurred in the Halls of Congress, Washington, D. C., Monday, February 23, 1848.

SEVENTH PRESIDENT, 1829-1837.
ANDREW JACKSON.

Was born in Mecklenberg County, North Carolina, Sunday, March 15, 1767, and was of Irish descent. He had meager educational advantages. He served in the Revolutionary War, and was once taken prisoner by the British. In 1785 he began to study law at Salisbury, North Carolina, and began first to practice at Nashville, Tenn., in 1788. In 1796 he was instrumental in passing the Constitution of Tennessee, and was sent to Congress from that State. He was a Judge of the Tennessee Supreme Court from 1798 to 1804. He took part in the War of 1812 with Great Britain, and in 1814 was appointed Major-General of the United States Army, commanding the American forces at the Battle of New Orleans. He also quelled the Seminole Indian outbreak in Florida 1817. His stubbornness of character won him the nickname of "Old Hickory." He was the first Governor of Florida in 1821. He was elected President in 1828, and again elected in 1832. His death occurred at Hermitage, near Nashville, Tenn., Sunday, June 8, 1845.

EIGHTH PRESIDENT, 1837-1841.

MARTIN VAN BUREN

Was born at Kinderhook, N. Y., Thursday, December 5, 1782. He was educated at the Kinderhook Academy, taking up the study of law and was admitted to the bar in 1803. At an early age he became interested in politics, and in 1812 he was elected to the Senate of New York. He was appointed Attorney-General of New York in 1815, and in 1816 was returned again to the State Senate. He became a United States Senator in 1821, and continued to hold that office till 1827. In 1829 he became Governor of New York, but soon afterwards resigned to become Secretary of State under Andrew Jackson. Three years later he became Vice President under Jackson, and in 1836 he was elected President of the United States. He was the first to propose the plan of an independent Treasury, which was finally adopted in 1840. It was during his term of office that the commercial crisis of 1837 occurred, in which all the banks suspended specie payment. His death occurred at Kinderhook, N. Y., Thursday, July 24, 1862.

NINTH PRESIDENT, 1841.

WILLIAM HENRY HARRISON.

Was the son of Benjamin Harrison, one of the signers of the Declaration of Independence. He was born in Berkeley, Virginia, Tuesday, February 9, 1773, and was educated in Hampden, Sidney College. It was his intention to enter the medical profession, but in 1791 he joined the army led by Wayne against the Indians in the Northwest. In this campaign he acted as ensign. In 1797 he left the army, and five years later was made Governor of the territory of Indiana. The nickname of "Tippecanoe," which he earned, was on account of his victory over the great Chief, Tecumseh, at a place called Tippecanoe. In 1813 he was made Major-General, and three years later was elected to Congress; in 1824 he was elected to the Senate, and later was sent as Ambassador to Colombia. The Whig Party nominated him to the presidency in 1836, but he was defeated. He was, however, elected to the presidency in 1840, but died the following year, a month after his inauguration. His death occurred at the White House, Washington, D. C., Sunday, April 4, 1841.

TENTH PRESIDENT, 1841-1845.

JOHN TYLER

Was born in Charles City County, Virginia, Monday, March 29, 1790, and at an early age practiced law. At the age of 21 he was elected to the State Legislature of Virginia, and was re-elected five times in succession. As a strong advocate of State Rights he entered Congress in 1816. In 1825 he occupied the chair of Governor of Virginia, and was returned to the United States Senate in 1827. He ran with Harrison for Vice President in 1840, was elected, and at the death of Harrison, on April 2, 1841, he became President. It was during his administration that Texas was annexed to the United States, and at the end of his official term he retired to private life; but with the breaking out of the Rebellion he sided with the Confederates, and was for a time a member of their Congress. His death occurred at the Ballard House, Richmond, Va., Friday, January 17, 1862.

ELEVENTH PRESIDENT, 1845-1849.

JAMES K. POLK

Was born in Mecklenburg County, North Carolina, Monday, November 2, 1795, and graduated from the University of that State. He was called to the bar in 1820, and three years later was elected to the Legislature of Tennessee. In 1825 he was a member of the United States Congress from that State. Ten years later he was chosen Speaker of the House of Representatives, and was also Speaker of Congress from 1837 to 1838. The year following he was elected Governor of Tennessee, and in 1844 was elected President of the United States. It was during his administration that the final consummation of annexation of Texas to the United States was made. His death occurred at Nashville, Tenn., Friday, June 15, 1849.

TWELFTH PRESIDENT, 1849-1850.
ZACHARY TAYLOR.

Was born in Orange County, Va., Tuesday November 24, 1784. In his early childhood he was taken to Louisville, Ky., where he grew up working on the home plantation. His education was of the simplest. He was appointed a Lieutenant in the United States Infantry in 1808, and two years later was promoted to a captaincy. In 1832 he served as a Colonel in a war against the Indian Chief, Black Hawk. He defeated the Seminoles, in Florida, in December, 1837, thus terminating the war. In the Mexican War he was sent to protect Texas, and laid siege to Monterey. He won the battle of Buena Vista. Was elected President in 1848, and died sixteen months after his inauguration. His death occurred at the White House, Washington, D. C., Tuesday, July 9, 1850.

THIRTEENTH PRESIDENT, 1850-1853.

MILLARD FILLMORE.

Was born at Summer Hill, in New York State, Tuesday, January 7, 1800. The only education he received was at a village school. At an early age he was apprenticed to a wool-carder, and while still a young man entered the law office of Judge Wood, who assisted him financially, and also assisted him in his law studies. In 1827 he was called to the bar, and two years later was elected to the New York Legislature. In 1832 he was elected to the United States Congress, and was subsequently re-elected three different times. In 1847 he was Comptroller of the State of New York, and one year later was elected Vice President of the United States. On account of the death of Zachary Taylor, he succeeded to the presidency the following year. His death occurred at Buffalo, N. Y., Sunday, March 9, 1874.

FOURTEENTH PRESIDENT, 1853-1857.

FRANKLIN PIERCE.

Was born at Hillsborough, New Hampshire, Friday, November 23, 1804. He graduated from Bowdoin College, Me., in the year 1824. Under Levi Woodbury he studied law, and was admitted to the bar in 1827. He practiced law at Hillsborough, his native town, and in 1833 was elected a member of Congress, four years later being returned to the United States Senate. He resigned in 1842 to take up again his legal profession at Concord, N. H. At the beginning of the Mexican War he entered the army as a private, and in 1847 was made Brigadier-General. He was elected President of the United States in 1852. It was under his administration that Jefferson Davis was appointed Secretary of War. During his term of office several important commercial treaties were consummated with foreign nations. His death occurred at Concord, N. H., Friday, October 8, 1869.

FIFTEENTH PRESIDENT, 1857-1861.

JAMES BUCHANAN.

Was born at Stony Batter, Franklin County, Pennsylvania, Saturday, April 23, 1791. It was at Dickinson College, Carlisle, that he received his education. After studying law he was admitted to the bar in 1812. Two years later he entered the Pennsylvania Legislature, and in 1820 he was chosen as a member of Congress. He remained there until 1831, when he was sent as Ambassador to Russia, a position which he occupied for three years. In 1833 he was elected United States Senator from Pennsylvania, and remained in the Senate until 1845, when he was appointed Secretary of State by President Polk. Some years later he retired to private life, and in 1853 he was appointed United States Minister to England. In 1856 he was elected President of the United States. His death occurred at Lancaster, Pennsylvania, Monday, June 1, 1868.

SIXTEENTH PRESIDENT, 1861-1865.
ABRAHAM LINCOLN.

Was born at Nolin Creek, Hardin County, Kentucky, Sunday, February 12, 1809. His ancestors were English Quakers. In 1816 his father moved to Indiana. For ten years Lincoln worked on the farm at home; his whole time at school did not exceed one year, but he was a voracious reader. In 1831 he helped to build a flat-boat on the Mississippi, on which he worked his way to New Orleans. On his return he became a clerk in a New Salem store. Two years later he became captain of volunteers. From 1834 to 1840 he was a member of the Illinois Legislature, where he was an acknowledged leader, in the meantime studying law. Springfield, Ill., was the first place where he began to practice law, in 1846. From 1849 to 1854 he practiced law, and was elected President of the United States in 1860; the following year the War of the Rebellion broke out. On September 22, 1862, he issued the memorable Emancipation Proclamation declaring the abolition of slavery. He was re-elected President in 1864; was assassinated on April 14, 1865, and died at Washington, D. C., April 15, 1865.

SEVENTEENTH PRESIDENT, 1865-1869.
ANDREW JOHNSON.

Was born at Raleigh, N. C., Thursday, December 29, 1808. He served ten years as an apprentice to a tailor, during which time he taught himself reading and writing. Some years later he was made Alderman of the village of Greenville, and in 1830 was elected Mayor, serving a term of three years. He was in the Legislature from 1835 to 1837, and again from 1839 to 1841. He was elected State Senator of Tennessee, and in 1843 was sent to the United States Congress, where he remained for ten years. At the end of this term he was elected Governor of Tennessee, and again in 1855 he served another term as Governor. He was United States Senator from 1857 to 1863, was Vice President under Lincoln, and at Lincoln's death succeeded to the presidency. He was impeached by the House in March, 1868, but was acquitted. His death occurred at Greenville, Tenn., Saturday, July 31, 1875.

EIGHTEENTH PRESIDENT, 1869-1877.
ULYSSES S. GRANT

Was born at Point Pleasant, Ohio, Saturday, April 27, 1822. In 1839 he entered the West Point Military Academy. In 1843 he was commissioned as a Second Lieutenant, and served in the Mexican War, under General Taylor. He was promoted to First Lieutenant in 1847, and served on the Pacific coast until 1854, when he resigned and lived on a farm for four years. Owing to bad health he gave up farming, and went into business in St. Louis. In 1860 he went into his father's store at Galena, Ill. When Lincoln called for troops in 1861, Grant drilled a company and took it to Springfield. On June 17th, he was made Colonel of the Twenty-first Illinois Infantry; shortly afterward he was promoted to Brigadier-General, and in 1864 was made Commander-in-Chief of the United States Armies. The rank of General was specially created for him in 1866. Two years later, in 1868, he was elected President, and again to a second term in 1872. His death occurred at Mt. McGregor, N. Y., Thursday, July 23, 1885.

NINETEENTH PRESIDENT, 1877-1881.
RUTHERFORD B. HAYES

Was born at Delaware, Ohio, Friday, October 4, 1822. He graduated from Kenyon College and from the School of Law at Harvard. In the year 1845 he began to practice at the bar in Lower Sandusky, Ohio, and was City Solicitor of Cincinnati from the year 1859 to 1861. At the breaking out of the Civil War he was appointed Major of the Twenty-third Ohio Infantry, and was shortly afterward promoted to the rank of Lieut.-Colonel. In the campaign of West Virginia he took a very prominent part, and was severely wounded at the battle of South Mountain. He was made Brigadier-General in 1864. Was elected to Congress for a while from 1864 to 1866. In 1868 he was elected Governor of Ohio, and again in 1876. In that year he was a Republican candidate for the presidency, and after a heated dispute over electoral votes, which were claimed by both parties, a Commission, appointed by Congress, gave the disputed votes to Hayes. He was President of the United States from 1877 to 1881. His death occurred at Fremont, Ohio, January 17, 1893.

TWENTIETH PRESIDENT, 1881.

JAMES A. GARFIELD

Was born at Bedford, Orange Township, Ohio, Saturday, November 19, 1831. His educational advantages were meager, being limited to a common-school education. Brought up on a farm, he was obliged to labor early and late, and at one time his employment consisted in driving a team of mules attached to a canal boat. He found time to study and by dint of perseverance he graduated at Williams College in the year 1856. Afterward he studied law and was admitted to the bar. From 1859 to 1860 he was a member of the Ohio Senate. In 1861 he entered the army as Colonel of the Forty-second Ohio Volunteers, and his promotion was rapid. From Brigadier-General he was made Chief-of-Staff in 1863, for gallantry at Chickamauga. Shortly afterward he was promoted to the rank of Major-General, but resigned to accept a seat in the 38th Congress. He was elected to the Senate in 1880, and the same year he was elected President of the United Stats. On July 2, 1881, h was assassinated, and died Monday, September 19, 1881, at Elberon, N. J.

TWENTY-FIRST PRESIDENT, 1881-1885.
CHESTER A. ARTHUR

Was born at Fairfield, Franklin County, Vermont, Tuesday, October 5, 1831. His ancestry was Scotch-Irish. He graduated from Union College, Schenectady, in 1849. Subsequently he studied law and was admitted to the Bar in 1851. He joined the Republican Party shortly after its first organization. He served as a staff officer of the State Militia of New York, and in 1861 he was appointed Inspector-General of the New York State National Guard and subsequently Quartermaster-General of the State troops. He was collector for the port of New York in 1871 and held this position until 1878. In 1880 he was elected Vice President of the United States, and on the death of President Garfield he succeeded to the Presidential chair. His death occurred in New York City, N. Y., Friday, November 18, 1886.

TWENTY-SECOND AND TWENTY-FOURTH PRESIDENT,

1885-1889.   1893-1897.

STEPHEN GROVER CLEVELAND

Was born at Caldwell, N. J., Saturday, March 18, 1837. When quite young his parents removed to Fayetteville, N. Y. He studied at the Clinton Academy, read law in Buffalo, was admitted to the Bar in 1859. He continued to practice law in Buffalo and in 1863 he was appointed Assistant District Attorney for Erie County. In 1869 he was made Sheriff of that County, and in 1874 was elected Mayor of Buffalo. In 1882 he was elected Governor of the State of New York, and two years later, in 1884, was elected President of the United States. He was nominated again in June, 1888, but was defeated by Benjamin Harrison. He was nominated the third time, in 1892, this time defeating Harrison, and gaining a second term as President of the United States.

TWENTY-THIRD PRESIDENT, 1889-1893.

BENJAMIN HARRISON.

Was born at North Bend, Ohio, Tuesday, August 20, 1833. He was a great-grandson of Benjamin Harrison, one of the signers of the Declaration of Independence, and grandson of the Ninth President of the United States. The year 1852 he graduated from the Miami University. He studied law in Cincinnati, and in 1854 removed to Indianapolis, Ind., where he began a legal practice which subsequently became very extensive. He joined the Union Army in 1862, and served until the close of the war, retiring to private life with the rank of Brevet Brigadier-General. He was defeated as Republican candidate for Governor of Indiana in the year 1876. Five years later he was elected to the United States Senate, where he served for six years. He was nominated by the Republican Party for President in 1888 and was elected President.

TWENTY-FIFTH PRESIDENT, 1897-1901.

WILLIAM McKINLEY

Was born at Niles, Trumbull County, Ohio, January 29, 1843; was educated in the public schools, Poland Academy, and Allegheny College; before attaining his majority he taught in the public schools; enlisted as a private in the Twenty-third Ohio Volunteer Infantry, June 11, 1861; promoted to Commissary-Sergeant April 15, 1862, to Second Lieutenant September 23, 1862, to First Lieutenant February 7, 1863, to Captain July 25, 1864; served successively on the staffs of Gens. R. B. Hayes, George Crook, and Winfield S. Hancock, and was brevetted Major in the United States Volunteers by President Lincoln for gallantry in battle March 13, 1865; detailed as acting Assistant Adjutant-General of the First Division, First Army Corps, on the staff of Gen. S. S. Carroll; mustered out of the service July 26, 1865; returning to civil life, he studied law in Mahoning County; took a course in the Albany (N. Y.) Law School, and in 1867 was admitted to the bar and settled at Canton, Ohio, which has since been his home; in 1869 he was elected Prosecuting Attorney of Stark County, and served a term in that office; in 1876 was elected a member of the National House of Representatives, and for fourteen years represented the Congressional district of which his county was a part. In 1896 he was elected President.

111

PATRIOTIC INFORMATION FOR THE LITTLE CITIZEN.

STATES AND TERRITORIES.	CAPITALS OF STATES AND TERRITORIES.	Population of States and Territories, 1890.	Population of Capitals, 1890.	WHEN ADMITTED INTO THE UNION. Anniversary Dates.	Numerical Order.	NICKNAMES APPLIED TO THE STATES.
Alabama	Montgomery	1,513,017	21,883	December 14, 1819	22	Cotton.
Arkansas	Little Rock	1,128,180	25,874	June 15, 1836	25	Bear.
California	Sacramento	1,208,130	26,386	September 9, 1850	31	Golden.
Colorado	Denver	419,200	106,713	August 1, 1876	38	Centennial.
Connecticut	Hartford	746,258	53,230	January 9, 1788	5	Land of Steady Habits.
Delaware	Dover	164,496	3,061	December 7, 1787	1	Diamond or Blue Hen.
Florida	Tallahassee	391,422	3,500	March 3, 1845	27	Peninsular.
Georgia	Atlanta	1,837,553	65,533	January 2, 1788	4	Empire State of the South.
Illinois	Springfield	3,826,351	24,963	December 3, 1818	21	Prairie or Sucker.
Indiana	Indianapolis	2,200,500	125,350	December 11, 1816	19	Hoosier.
Iowa	Des Moines	1,911,900	50,093	December 28, 1846	29	Hawkeye.
Idaho	Boise City	84,385	5,000	July 3, 1890	40	Mineral. [Flower.
Kansas	Topeka	1,427,100	31,007	January 29, 1861	34	Garden of the West and Sun
Kentucky	Frankfort	1,860,650	7,892	June 1, 1792	15	Corn Cracker and Blue Grass.
Louisiana	Baton Rouge	1,120,600	10,578	April 30, 1812	18	Creole and Pelican.
Maine	Augusta	661,100	10,527	March 15, 1820	23	Pine Tree.
Maryland	Annapolis	1,100,390	7,605	April 28, 1788	7	Old Line.
Massachusetts	Boston	2,238,948	448,447	February 6, 1788	6	Baked Beans and Old Colony.
Michigan	Lansing	2,100,900	13,102	January 26, 1837	26	Lake.
Minnesota	St. Paul	1,301,826	133,156	May 11, 1858	32	North Star and Gopher.
Mississippi	Jackson	1,299,600	5,920	December 10, 1817	20	Bayou.
Missouri	Jefferson City	2,679,184	6,742	August 10, 1821	24	Puke and Iron.
Montana	Helena	132,159	13,834	February 22, 1889	39	Silver.
Nebraska	Lincoln	1,058,940	55,154	March 1, 1867	37	Blackwater.
Nevada	Carson City	45,761	4,000	October 31, 1864	36	Sage Brush.
New Hampshire	Concord	376,630	17,004	June 21, 1788	9	Granite.
New Jersey	Trenton	1,444,933	57,458	December 13, 1787	3	Garden.
New York	Albany	6,000,000	94,923	July 26, 1788	11	Empire.
North Carolina	Raleigh	1,617,947	12,678	November 21, 1789	12	Old North.
North Dakota	Bismarck	182,719	2,180	February 22, 1889	39	Prolific.
Ohio	Columbus	3,672,316	88,150	January 19, 1803	17	Buckeye.
Oregon	Salem	313,767	10,422	February 14, 1859	33	Web-foot and Beaver.
Pennsylvania	Harrisburg	5,258,114	39,385	December 12, 1797	2	Keystone.
Rhode Island	Providence	345,506	132,146	May 29, 1790	13	Little Rhody.
South Carolina	Columbia	1,151,150	15,353	May 23, 1788	8	Palmetto.

PATRIOTIC INFORMATION FOR THE LITTLE CITIZEN.—Continued.

STATES AND TERRITORIES.	CAPITALS OF STATES AND TERRITORIES.	Population of States and Territories, 1890.	Population of Capitals, 1890.	WHEN ADMITTED INTO THE UNION. ANNIVERSARY DATES.	Numerical Order.	NICKNAMES APPLIED TO THE STATES.
South Dakota	Pierre	328,808	3,235	February 22, 1889	39	Granary of America.
Tennessee	Nashville	1,767,518	76,168	June 1, 1796	16	Volunteer.
Texas	Austin	2,235,523	14,575	December 29, 1845	28	Lone Star.
Utah	Salt Lake City	207,905	44,843	In the session of 1894 Congress passed an act enabling Utah to become a State July 4, 1896.		Mormons.
Vermont	Montpelier	332,422	5,000	March 4, 1791	14	Green Mountain.
Virginia	Richmond	1,655,980	81,388	June 25, 1788	10	Old Dominion.
Washington	Olympia	349,390	4,700	February 22, 1889	39	Big Trees.
West Virginia	Wheeling	762,794	34,522	June 19, 1863	35	Switzerland of America.
Wisconsin	Madison	1,686,880	13,426	May 29, 1848	30	Badger.
Wyoming	Cheyenne	60,705	11,690	July 10, 1890	41	National Park.
Alaska Territory	Sitka	49,850		Purchased from Russia Oct. 18, 1867.		Gadsden Purchase.
Arizona	Prescott	59,620	1,800	Purchased from Mexico in 1853.		Horned Toad.
District of Columbia	Washington	230,392	230,392	Created the capital in 1791.		Capital United States.
Indian Territory	Tahlequah	186,390	1,350	Purchased from the Province of Louisiana in 1832 as a reservation for Indian tribes.		
New Mexico	Santa Fe	153,593	6,185	Organized September, 1850.		Red Man's Home. Sheep Ranch.
Oklahoma	Guthrie	61,834	7,714	Opened April 19, 1892		Cycloners.

REMARKS.—Every school should celebrate the anniversary of the admittance of their State into the Union with exercises bearing upon the history of their native or adopted State.

www.ingramcontent.com/pod-product-compliance
Lightning Source LLC
Chambersburg PA
CBHW030405170426
43202CB00010B/1500

*9 7 8 3 3 3 7 3 0 6 4 8 9 *